Ken TAYLOR

BRINGING THE BIBLE TO LIFE

JIM KRAUS

BARBOUR
PUBLISHING

© 2006 by Barbour Publishing, Inc.

ISBN 1-59310-702-1

Scripture quotations marked KJV are taken from the King James Version of the Bible.

Scripture quotations marked NLT are taken from the *Holy Bible*, New Living Translation, copyright © 1996. Used by permission of Tyndale House Publishers, Inc. Wheaton, Illinois 60189, U.S.A. All rights reserved.

Cover illustration © Dick Bobnick
Cover design by Douglas Miller (mhpubarts.com)

Published by Barbour Publishing, Inc., P.O. Box 719, Uhrichsville, OH 44683, www.barbourbooks.com

Our mission is to publish and distribute inspirational products offering exceptional value and biblical encouragement to the masses.

eCpa Member of the
Evangelical Christian
Publishers Association

Printed in the United States of America.
5 4 3 2 1

PROLOGUE

1940

Twenty-three-year-old Ken Taylor sat alone in his small room at the Montreal YMCA. He was struggling with his message he was to give that night at the InterVarsity meeting at McGill University.

I just don't understand this section in Ephesians, he said to himself. *I know it's my topic tonight, but I just don't get it.*

He read the passage again slowly, a verse at a time. He scowled. He was still confused. He couldn't see the significance of the verses or apply them to his life—let alone the lives of the students he was to teach that evening.

Suddenly Ken sat back in the chair and stared out the small window.

It's always been like this, he said to himself dejectedly. He saw all of his Bible reading the same way—a struggle to understand the meaning. He shook his head, thinking that such understanding came easily to other people.

Some of his friends seemed to glory in Bible reading.

"Why can't I?"

He stood up, frustrated. "Why can't somebody translate the Bible so a person like me can understand it?"

ONE

The Early Years

W hy, Kenneth has always been a Christian," Ken's mother said to a friend. "He and his older brother, Douglas. . .well, they have always believed." She was having tea with her friend in the parlor of the Taylor home in Seattle, Washington. The year was 1922. Little Kenneth was five years old.

Ken overheard his mother that day, and had he been asked, he would have agreed with her. He could not remember a specific time when his father, a pastor in the Presbyterian Church, sat down with Doug and him and told them that they couldn't get to heaven unless they said just the right words of faith. Instead, his parents assumed that their two sons loved Jesus as much as they did.

The way of salvation was clear to both boys, having heard it often during family devotions and as their father explained the Bible text to them. They also heard him preach it from the pulpit on Sundays.

Sometimes, with some measure of embarrassment, Ken would listen as his father told people he met that Jesus died on the cross for their salvation. Ken wanted so much to be smooth and assured like his father—but he was plagued by a degree of timidity and fear.

That timid nature may have started when Ken was only three and a half years old.

It was moving day.

Ken's family was moving from his birthplace in Portland to their new home in Seattle, taking the train.

It was a hot, sultry day, and Ken and Doug walked down the aisle as the train car gently rocked on the tracks. They were getting drinks at the watercooler at the far end of the coach. The boys were having fun, making the trip back and forth, laughing and giggling to each other.

All of a sudden, a large man sitting near the watercooler barked at them angrily, "You children! Stop this nonsense. Go back to your seats and don't come back up here again. This is for grown-ups, not foolish, disrespectful children!"

Ken and Doug scurried back to their seats without saying a word. Ken sat on his seat for the rest of the journey, terrified that he had done something very, very wrong, and would not move again until the train had come to the Seattle station.

Years later, Ken often thought back to this incident. *Could it have caused my sense of timidity? Could a life be altered by a single event such as that?*

Ken was troubled by such fears throughout his early childhood. One of his worst fears was that his mother would run away if he continued to misbehave.

Another small incident in Ken's early life also impacted him for years.

The Taylor family was sitting in the parlor of their home, which was reserved for greeting guests and special occasions. It was there that their ornate family Bible was kept. It was always open—and well used. A guest rose from the couch, and as he did so, he brushed the Bible with his leg.

The Bible tumbled to the floor with a great *thump*.

Ken's father practically dove for the Bible, gently picking it up, nearly cradling it in his hands as he replaced it in its original position. He didn't say a word—it was an accident, after all—but the concern on his face left a mark on young Ken.

"He had such a deep respect for the Word of God and its Author," Ken said later in life.

That respect helped guide the young man and reminded him to keep the Bible in an important place in his life.

Years later, Ken would tell that story and remark, "How grateful I am for such a godly heritage."

Despite his godly heritage and upbringing, Ken occasionally found himself in trouble. One incident in particular was etched in Ken's memory.

Ken was six years old, he recalled, when he attempted to play a foolish prank on his family. He awoke early one summer morning while the rest of the family was still asleep.

"I'm going to play a trick on them—and hide where

no one can find me," he said.

Silently, he slipped downstairs and entered the parlor, still in his pajamas. He waited until he heard movement upstairs. He crept behind the large davenport in the parlor and held his breath, giggling to himself over the wonderful trick he was playing.

Ken could tell by the way the stairs creaked that his father was the first one up. He heard dishes rattling in the kitchen, and later the rest of the family awoke.

After a few minutes, Mr. Taylor asked Doug, "Where's Ken? Is he still asleep?"

Doug must have looked surprised. "Ken's not upstairs. The bedroom is empty," he said.

The family panicked—Ken was missing!

"Kenneth!" his mother shouted from the porch, thinking he must have walked outside and wandered off.

Doug took off and began to search the neighborhood. His father ran outside for a moment, then hurried back inside. He picked up the phone and dialed the number for the police.

"My son," he exclaimed, "he's only six, and he's missing!"

All the while, Ken began to grow more and more uneasy—his wonderful prank had taken on a most unsettling turn.

Minutes seemed to grow long, and finally Ken gathered the courage to crawl out from his hiding place and call for his father.

His father was not angry like he had expected and feared—but instead was greatly relieved. All he said was that he was surprised that Ken had heard all the commotion but continued to hide.

His mother greeted him with great relief as well.

After all had settled down, his mother spoke to him sternly yet lovingly. "Honestly, Kenneth, I don't know what possessed you to do what you did today. You hold on to bad ideas too long. Someday you'll remember this. I hope it keeps you out of trouble."

Both Ken and Doug grew up with a strong sense of right and wrong—reinforced by their father's stern moral conscience.

When Ken was in the second grade, each child brought in a dime to purchase a small booklet about the history of the school.

"Children, I have dimes from every one of you," Miss Mott explained to her class. "And everyone has a booklet. Now I want everyone to turn to page sixteen."

The class was filled with the sound of rustling pages.

"Does anyone have a star pasted in the margin?"

Ken's hand shot up excitedly. "I do, Miss Mott!" he exclaimed.

"You're our lucky student today," she said. "You get your dime back!"

Ken was delighted and was the envy of the class.

When he returned home from school that day, he told his father the news.

". . .and I got my dime back. Do you want to see it?" he proudly asked.

His father's stern face told Ken all he needed to know.

"Ken," he said gravely, "what happened today in class was a form of gambling. No son of mine will ever gamble.

You must take the dime back to Miss Mott tomorrow."
Ken did so with great reluctance but with obedience.

Mr. Taylor passed on aspects of his creativity to his
sons. He told them of an event that occurred before
he was married when he was traveling as a salesman.
He noticed in all the churches he attended how little
of the churches' money went to foreign missions. He
also noticed that much of the budget of the average
church was made up of only a few wealthy families. He
kept pondering those facts and wondered if it would
help to have all the members of a church sign a pledge
at the beginning of the year, announcing their level of
support. The more he prayed about the idea, the better
it sounded.

"But what could I do?" he asked his sons. "I was just
a simple, uneducated traveling salesman."

In spite of this, the idea wouldn't leave him. He
met with the Presbyterian denominational leaders, who
seemed enthusiastic about the idea. Eventually, he met with
Henry Crowell, chairman of the Quaker Oats Company
and a very influential lay leader of the Presbyterian
Church.

"Mr. Crowell liked the idea so much that he
presented it to the leadership of the church," Mr. Taylor
explained. "And they even used my title when they
implemented it throughout the church—'The Every
Member Campaign.'"

Once started, the initiative gave foreign missions a
great economic boost.

Ken recalled this story later in life, wondering if his
father's initiative was what instilled in him the ability to

observe a need, analyze it, pray about it, and finally act upon it.

It was a cold winter day, gray and raining, typical of Seattle weather. Ken's father stood before a classroom filled with the children of the church. He often led Sunday school for the children.

He walked to the blackboard and drew a line down the center of it. Then he drew a cross in the middle.

He began to speak about heaven and wrote the word *heaven* on one side of the board. Underneath, he wrote words like *angels*, *happiness*, *God*, and *love*.

"What's the opposite of heaven?" he asked.

Someone answered, "Hell."

He wrote the word *hell* on the other side of the board, then added words like *sin*, *Satan*, and *death*. Then he turned to the class and stared at them for a long moment.

"Which side do you want to be on?" he whispered. "Jesus died on the cross for you. Do you want Him as your Savior, to give you all the good things and save you from the evil ones?"

Several students nodded in affirmation.

"I know what I have chosen," Mr. Taylor said boldly. "I have chosen Jesus."

Then he wrote his initials on the side of the board under heaven.

"Any one of you children can make that choice now. Here's the chalk. Initial the board with your name. Make the right choice."

Over the years, he taught the same lesson again and again. Both Ken and his brother wrote their initials under the word *heaven*. Despite this, Ken never felt that he had inherited his father's gift for sharing his faith.

"It came so easy to him," Ken explained, "and I was always tongue-tied when I had the opportunity."

One other activity that his father engaged in also had a lasting impact on Ken throughout his life.

As part of his tithe, once a week Mr. Taylor placed a small, five-inch ad in the *Queen Anne News*, a local newspaper.

He would sit at the typewriter and tap out a story. The titles were always eye-catching, like "Man Bites Dog." Then he would share the gospel in clear, easy-to-understand terminology. He always ran the ads on the sports pages—and tried to make them look as much like actual news articles as possible.

"Why the sports pages?" Ken asked his father.

"Because these stories are aimed at men—and I know most men read the sports pages."

He would write for several hours, getting the message just right—and then work for hours more getting it to fit into that small, five-inch space. He would write, scratch words out, and write again.

"It's called editing, Ken. I don't have much space, so I want to use just the right words. You know, Ken, if the apostle Paul were alive today, he would use the newspapers to reach millions."

TWO

Growing Up

When Ken was seven years old, the family moved from Seattle to Beaverton, Oregon. His father accepted a position as fund-raiser for Albany College, a Presbyterian institution at the time. The college was located near Portland. He also became part-time pastor of the Beaverton Congregational Church.

Ken enjoyed the atmosphere of the small town, with its wooden sidewalks and neighbors who raised chickens.

Beaverton reflected the standards of the nation at the time: Movies were free from profanity and explicit sex, divorce was rare, and the magazines at Dean's Drug Store were suitable for just about everyone. There was one store that carried dime novels—sensational stories with lurid covers—but Ken was not allowed to read them; nor would he have chosen to even if he had been allowed.

Illegal drugs were unknown in the small town. And even without Prohibition, alcohol was not used very much—although a few older boys said they knew of speakeasies in Portland where a man could find hard liquor if he knew who to ask for.

One day Ken's mother mused, "I hope you boys never learn to smoke."

Ken was astounded by her remark. How could she ever dream that he would betray her in that way? *Tobacco? Never!*

Dancing was the rage of the day—especially ballroom dancing—but Ken's church and his family were dead set against it. Square dancing was permitted by some "liberal" churches, but it was often called "folk games" to avoid using the word *dancing*.

"Why can't we dance?" Ken asked his father one day—even though he had no desire to learn how to do it. He was simply curious.

"Well, son, I don't think it's proper for one man's wife to be in another man's arms—no matter how innocent they claim it to be."

"What if they're not married?" he asked.

"Then they're enjoying physical contact that should be saved until marriage."

Ken looked puzzled. His father realized that he had no idea of what that actually meant.

"Maybe your mother and I are overdoing this part of your education—your moral education, so to speak. But I don't think we are. I'm trying to save you from a lot of potential pain and evil."

Ken nodded, but he still had questions.

"You know I pray for you and your brother every night," Mr. Taylor continued. "And I specifically ask that God will save you from the moment of sin that could ruin your entire life. That's what I pray."

Ken nodded, still not sure what that meant exactly, but he was grateful for the prayer. It would protect him his entire life—and God would answer his father's prayer.

"Boys, we only have ten minutes left until you have to go to school," Ken's mother called out. "You'd better get downstairs now. We're ready for our time with the Bible."

Ken and Doug hurried down the stairs and took their usual seats.

Their father waited until they were settled and then began reading. Today it was from Malachi in the Old Testament. Ken listened and tried to pay close attention. In some ways, he was always relieved when the Bible reading stopped and their prayer time began. At least he could understand the prayers.

His father's words rang in his ears. "If you boys don't get God's Word deep into your hearts and do what it tells you to do, you'll never amount to much for God."

Ken knew his father was correct, but he still struggled. The Bible was hard to understand. The only version they used then was the King James Version, and the centuries-old language was strange to his ears.

What made Ken's inner confusion even more intense was that Doug seemed to get the meanings easily and quickly. In fact, he had declared at age six that he was going to be a missionary to Tibet. Even in school, Doug had the habit of bowing his head and closing his eyes. From where Ken sat, he could tell that his brother was praying about something.

One day, the teacher came beside Doug's desk and

noticed his closed eyes. She asked Ken if Doug was ill, and Ken just gulped and said his brother was probably just resting his eyes.

Ken was greatly relieved that she let it go at that.

As they grew up, God protected Ken and Doug, sometimes in small ways and sometimes in larger ways.

One summer, the Taylors were on a family vacation on an island in Puget Sound, and Ken and Doug found a raft on the beach in front of their cabin. They looked around and saw no one nearby, so they decided to take it out into the chilly waters.

They paddled about in the shallow water, laughing and splashing.

"Doug, we're getting pretty far from shore," Ken said as he noticed the cabins growing smaller.

"It's okay," Doug said. "We'll just paddle back."

Both boys began to paddle and soon discovered that they were making little headway against a hidden current.

Their mother sat up on the beach and called out, "Boys, come back closer!"

"We're trying!" came their frantic reply.

The tide was rushing out and carrying them with it.

Mrs. Taylor waded into the water as far as she could, then began swimming toward them. She seemed exhausted when she got there, and she rested a bit. "We have to make it back to shore," she exclaimed breathlessly. She started kicking as hard as she could. Both Ken and Doug tried to help, but they realized their splashing wasn't making any difference. It was their mother's strong, determined swimming that returned them safely to the shore.

Once they all got their feet on land again, Ken

thanked God aloud for his mother's strength to get them all back to safety.

Because of their father's work at the church, Ken and Doug were exposed at an early age to missions and overseas ministry. Missionaries from Africa, China, and South America were visitors in their home. Their stories and struggles made their work come alive to Ken. He gladly offered his dimes in Sunday school to support their efforts.

One time, Ken encountered a less-than-noble response to his and his family's prayers for missionaries.

Ken's father had heard about a missionary in India, and the family committed to praying for them every day.

"Do they know we're praying for them?" Ken asked his father.

Mr. Taylor looked puzzled for a moment, then answered. "No. I don't think they do."

That evening, Ken watched as his father penned a long letter to these missionaries, explaining how the family prayed for them regularly.

Some time later, Ken ran into the house holding a letter filled with strange stamps.

"I think it's from India!" he exclaimed.

His father opened the letter and began to scowl as he read it.

"What's the matter?" Ken asked.

"Pshaw," he said, which was as close as he would ever come to profanity. "He said not to write him anymore unless we sent some money. He said even a dollar would have helped. And if we don't send money, he doesn't have time to write back."

Ken was disappointed. The rest of the family continued to pray for them, despite the negative letter, but Ken didn't. Eventually, that missionary was mentioned less and less often.

Yet one sour experience did not negate the duty to be concerned about the world's need for the gospel.

When missionaries on furlough stopped for a visit, Ken often yearned to help them and to spread the Good News about Jesus. Perhaps because of that early exposure to missionaries, Ken, in later years, would devote much of his time and resources to missionary efforts. His brother was encouraged as well, and Doug spent many years as a medical missionary in Africa.

Not only did his father and missionaries shape young Ken—other dedicated teachers did, too.

Sunday school, especially for a pastor's son, was nearly mandatory. Most children in the neighborhood went, too.

"Mr. Doty," Ken said as he walked into the classroom one Sunday, "here's my dime for the missionaries."

Mr. Doty smiled warmly and placed the young boy's offering in a special box. He could tell that Ken was growing spiritually. He never missed an opportunity to share what he had with others and always happily gave his tithe, which was not always the case with other children. If they could have figured out a way to hold on to their dimes, he was certain they would have tried.

"Children," Mr. Doty called out, "we have a special guest today, and I want you all to pay close attention to him. This is Mr. Nunn from the Pocket Testament League."

Mr. Nunn, a small man with a large valise, shuffled

to the front of the class and waited until the children settled down. It was not often that a visitor was in class.

"Now," Mr. Nunn began, almost nervous, "how many of you know what a Testament is?"

A few children raised their hands.

"It's the Bible," one said.

"No. . .it's half the Bible," said another.

Mr. Nunn smiled. "You're both sort of correct. The Bible is made up of two sections—the Old Testament and the New Testament. The New Testament is the story about Jesus and His disciples."

"Do you children think it's a good idea to read about Jesus?"

The class murmured in agreement.

"Well, I have a free gift for every one of you, then."

Ken was excited. Not only did the class have a visitor, but the visitor came bearing presents!

"But there is one catch to this gift."

Several children couldn't hold back their moans of disappointment.

"It's not a bad thing. Really."

Mr. Nunn reached into his valise and extracted a small book. He held it over his head.

"This, children, is the entire New Testament of the Bible. And I want to give each of you a copy. It's totally free—but you have to promise me one thing in order to receive your free gift."

"What? What?" came the excited replies.

"You have to promise me and God that you will read the New Testament each and every day. You have to promise."

The children responded with great enthusiasm and

eagerly lined up to get their free copies.

Ken took his book home and read some of it that very afternoon. It wasn't easy for him, but a promise was a promise.

He kept trying to keep his promise of daily reading. But if he had kept track, he admitted later, he probably broke his vow about 300 out of the next 365 days.

"I just don't understand it," he complained to his brother one night. "I did better in the four Gospels. Things happen there, and I can follow it. The book of Acts, I understand, pretty much. But once I go farther than that, the meanings get all muddled and I don't get much out of it."

Doug gave him a quizzical look. "It all makes sense to me," he replied.

Ken's brother seemed to understand everything. His parents seemed to have no difficulty with the Bible and actually reveled in the process of studying it. Ken figured his parents liked it because they had been reading it their entire lives, but he almost became angry with Doug, and a little jealous, because he was getting so much more from his Bible reading than Ken was from his.

It was an emotion that would later fuel his career.

"But you've always been a Christian," Doug whispered to Ken.

"I know. But I never went forward like this," Ken responded.

The two of them were at church. Ken was twelve years old. They were participating in the Sunday evening youth meeting.

Mr. Doty, the faithful sponsor of the group, stood up in front. "Are you sure you're a Christian?" he asked, his tone friendly but hinting at an urgency. "You know that no one else can make this decision for you. It doesn't matter if your mother and father are Christians. They can't get you into heaven. Each one of you has to make that decision on your own. You each have to accept or reject Jesus Christ, who died for your sins."

Mr. Doty let his words sink in.

"Do you remember when you made that decision?" he asked. "Do you remember the specific moment?"

Ken shook his head. He could not recall a time of decision. He had "always been a Christian."

"Well, if you can't remember the exact time—and that's fine—I have a suggestion. If you want to be sure that you have made that decision, or if you want to make that decision right now, tonight—then I want you to stand up now."

Ken's heart was beating fast, and he gulped once, then stood up. He looked around, and several others joined him in standing up that evening.

Ken's public testimony was an important event in his life, one that he would recall when anyone asked him about his "big decision."

Being a Christian was taken seriously in the Taylor household, and part of their faith consisted of observing the Ten Commandments.

That observance included Sunday restrictions in honor of the Sabbath. No one went to the store on Sunday—no matter what they might run out of. If they didn't have it, they simply made do without it. They didn't stop at gas stations—so trips had to be carefully planned. They would not work that day—not even shining their shoes; they did that Saturday night. They did not play sports, swim, or mow the lawn on Sunday, either.

Taking walks or drives to visit with friends, reading, and playing board games were things they could do on Sunday.

No one talked much about the rules—it was just something the entire family understood. Some things you did on Sunday, and others you did not.

One Sunday afternoon, the family was camping by a lake, and the sun beat down on them. Mr. Taylor wiped his brow and suggested that they all go to the beach and cool off by going for a "quiet swim."

Ken recalled being shocked by his father's violation of one of the traditional taboos!

THREE

High School

S on, when you start your classes, I want you to look up a student who will be in school with you."

Ken looked up from his book.

"What's his name?"

"*Her* name," his father replied, "is Margaret West. I know her father. They say he's a millionaire."

Ken wondered what the daughter of a millionaire might be like. But in the rush of the first few days of school, he forgot all about his father's request. Later, he asked a friend if he knew who Margaret West was. His friend pointed her out—she was sitting a few rows away.

Ken thought, *She seems nice. . .and she's pretty, too.* He made his way over to her and introduced himself. She hadn't heard of him, but thirteen-year-olds do not stand on ceremony, and they chatted for a while.

Some weeks later, Ken's father asked if he had met Margaret West. Ken said that he had.

"Well, I was mistaken about her father. Someone said

he was rich, but bad investments nearly wiped them out."

Ken wondered if Margaret knew about that, as well.

During Ken's freshman year, he gained weight and grew several inches. The football coach thought he might be a prime candidate for the team. But to the disappointment of both Ken and the coach, Ken's father would not agree to allow him to participate. He was unwilling to let Ken risk injury.

"Sorry, Ken, but that's my decision," Mr. Taylor said firmly.

Ken did not try to argue with him. They both assumed that the father knew best.

Instead of football, Ken tried a sport that was deemed less dangerous.

"Hey, Ken," called out one of his friends in school, "they're organizing a two-mile cross-country race over lunch."

"So?"

"You ought to race," his friend continued. "You're fast. I've seen you run."

"But I have never run before. . . . I mean in competition."

"You never know unless you try."

Ken borrowed a pair of gym shoes—that almost fit. At the sound of the gun, he was off, running through brush, around trees, and on country roads. The course circled around twice and was set to finish on the football field.

To his surprise, nearing the end of the second circuit, Ken looked back and did not see anyone close to him. Even more surprisingly, he finished first! Coach Warren promptly invited Ken to join the track team and run the mile. Ken did, and he proceeded to win his full share of points in track meets with other schools.

"Hey, Ken," said one of his friends in the freshman class, "you ought to come to the Frasers' with me."

"Frasers'? You mean Mr. and Mrs. Fraser?"

"Yep. They host a Bible study for high school kids on Saturday night. I've been going for a couple of weeks."

Ken debated attending or not, unsure of what to expect.

"Margaret comes most nights."

"Margaret West?"

"Yep."

The next Saturday night found Ken and a large group of high school students crowded into the living room of Mr. and Mrs. Gordon Fraser. Ken was impressed with Mrs. Fraser's warm and gracious welcome—and with Mr. Fraser's thoughtful and well-presented exposition of Bible prophecy.

Ken soon became a regular at the Bible study. He relished the camaraderie, the happy times of fellowship, the learning, the singing, and the hot cider and donuts afterwards! He knew, even then, that this was a key stepping-stone in his spiritual growth and outlook. It was good for him to see that other kids his age loved the Lord and that adults other than his parents were committed to their spiritual maturity.

Besides the impact of his parents, Ken pointed to this group as one of the highest and strongest influences on his life.

One day, Ken remained home from school, suffering

from a high fever. It was unusual for him to be ill, and his mother brought him soup and sympathy. He even decided that he was too sick to attend the social being held by the youth group at church that evening.

After school, his brother came into his room and asked him, "How ya feeling?"

"Not so good. How was school? Did I miss anything?"

Doug shrugged. "Not much. A pop quiz in history. It was pretty easy. All about the War of 1812."

"Anything else?"

Doug thought for a moment. "Oh, yes. You know Bob Denney, right?"

Ken nodded. Bob was a close friend, and Ken considered him to be an honorable fellow.

"Well, Bob invited Margaret to the social tonight."

Ken sat up in bed but tried to hide his surprise. "Margaret West? To the social tonight?"

Doug offered a curious look in return. "Well, sure. What did you think?"

Doug left the room, and Ken sat alone for a while, becoming more and more agitated about having to miss the social. He was sure that it wasn't that he objected to Margaret's going with Bob. After all, his friendship with Margaret had not progressed to the point of his having any exclusive claim on Margaret. But he did feel sad that he wouldn't be there to enjoy being near her. The more he thought about it, the less sick he felt. Shakily, he got out of bed, took a shower, and dressed.

His mother came to his room with more soup. "Where are you going?" she asked.

"To the social," Ken answered evenly.

"But you're sick."

"Well, I feel much better now."

Mrs. Taylor responded with a puzzled look of awareness, apparently not totally deceived, but she did not stand in Ken's way.

Ken went to the party, feeling better all the time, especially since he got to be near Margaret that evening.

"But why do I need to take a course in public speaking?" Ken asked his father.

"I think it's a good skill to have," Mr. Taylor answered. "As a pastor, public speaking is perhaps the most important skill to have—aside from Bible knowledge, that is."

"I know it may be useful, but it makes me nervous to get up in front of people and talk to them."

"I know, son, but you'll be more useful to the Lord if you learn to do it well."

"But some people have talent for speaking, and some don't," Ken objected.

"If you don't, you can learn."

Ken recognized the final words of a discussion when he heard them. He would sign up for public speaking as his father desired.

Ken found himself in Mr. Webb's public speaking class, and contrary to his father's thinking, he never quite got over his nervousness. Yet despite that nervousness, he also signed up for the freshman debate team—with a senior class partner, Ivan Bierly. Ivan was a natural speaker, smooth and confident, and Ken observed him and learned.

The following year, Ken had a new debate partner—

Margaret West. She was inexperienced in debate, but she was a natural leader.

"Margaret," Ken said over the phone one Sunday, "I think we should get together this afternoon to review our upcoming debate material."

Margaret seemed a bit surprised, but happy enough for Ken to come over.

In the entire year that Ken and Ivan were partners, they never once met on a Sunday for review. But this was different, Ken told himself. He walked the two and a half miles to her home, and they sat in the parlor, poring over debate material and discussing strategies.

At the end of their high school term, the Debate Club tradition was to hold a banquet to honor all those who participated during the year.

"Will you be going, Margaret?" Ken asked.

"Of course," she replied.

Parents were invited to attend, as well, so Ken asked the next question, "Will your folks be there?"

"No, they can't make it. I'm going alone," Margaret replied.

Ken thought hard for a moment. "Want me to pick you up on the way?" he asked.

"Sure," she replied. "What time?"

It was settled. They had a date. Well, perhaps it was more accurate to say Ken's family had a date. Ken's parents and brother were also going.

The day of the banquet came, and Doug was late returning with the family car. Ken paced the floor, growing more and more anxious until Doug arrived fifteen minutes late.

When the Taylors arrived at Margaret's house, she

was ready—looking beautiful and composed. She seemed a bit surprised by the attendance of Ken's family, but she eased Ken's tension with her cheerfulness and poise.

It was a good evening—for their first official date.

Ken had aspired to be class valedictorian for the class of 1934. But the class, with faculty approval, voted to have four speakers that graduation night—including both Ken and Margaret.

Ken sat on the stage and looked out over the crowd—fellow students, parents, relatives, faculty. It was a bittersweet moment, almost traumatic. The sky that afternoon had turned a crimson red, and Ken felt like this moment was the end of the world. He thought that life would never again be so sweet, but he soon learned that the best was yet to come.

FOUR

Preparing for College

"So, Ken, will you be getting a job after high school?" asked an older man from church. "I hear they're hiring down at the shipyards."

Ken shook his head. "No, I'm going to college."

The man looked surprised. "A healthy boy like you? You could make good money using your arms and legs."

"No. . .my father. . .well, I guess he always assumed that his sons would go to school. He said he didn't have the chance, and his lack of credentials was one of his regrets. Both Doug and I are going to college."

"You don't say. Have you decided where to go?"

At first, Ken had planned to go to Oregon State, but one Sunday evening had changed his mind. "I'm going to Wheaton College."

"Wheaton College? Where's that? I never heard of it."

"It's in Wheaton, Illinois. Not too far from Chicago."

"Chicago? But. . .that's almost across the whole country!"

Ken smiled. Until a few weeks ago, he would have agreed with the man's geographic assessment. But a gospel team of athletes from Wheaton College changed his mind when they passed through Portland and stopped to minister at Central Bible Church, where the Taylors had been attending for several years. Everyone who attended the service spoke of the inspiring stories from the team and of the sincerity of their testimonies. The young men all spoke eloquently about how and why they had become Christians.

Ken recalled how enthusiastic they all seemed about their school and how they encouraged all the young people in the congregation to consider sending an application to Wheaton College.

"But Wheaton?" one of his friends had commented. "That's way back East."

Doug applied first, and since the brothers had been side by side since the first grade, Ken decided to apply, as well—though he was more than a little reluctant to leave his home, friends, and familiar surroundings.

A few weeks later, two letters came in the mail—one for Doug, one for Ken. They both had been accepted at Wheaton!

The tuition for each semester would cost seventy-five dollars. There were no men's dormitories, but rooms in private homes were available near the campus. Room rates ranged from $1.75 to $2.00 per week per person.

Students could travel from Portland to Wheaton by riding with other students from the Portland area. The average car-share rate for a one-way trip was fifteen dollars per passenger—gas cost only twenty-three cents per gallon in those days.

Both boys spent the summer of 1934 trying to raise money for the expenses of their first term at Wheaton. They worked first at a flower farm—hoeing, watering, planting, and digging bulbs for thirty cents an hour.

Ken also worked at another farm, lifting hay bales and piling them onto horse-drawn wagons. The hours were long, and the work was hard, hot, and dusty. Wages there began at nineteen cents, but with experience and promotions, a worker could progress up to thirty-five cents an hour.

Summer drew to a close, and there was a round of farewell parties and final get-togethers throughout the neighborhood and with church friends.

When the day arrived for them to leave for school, both Ken and Doug were excited. But their father and mother did not feel quite the same. Mrs. Taylor was quiet and solemn, clasping her hands together. Mr. Taylor tried to appear cheerful, but he was poorly concealing his true feelings.

The Taylors arrived at a friend's home from where they would depart to Wheaton. They began to load up the car, but as they worked, Ken saw his father walk to the end of the street and back, all alone. Everyone was sensitive to Mr. Taylor's feelings. Ken realized that he was crying out to God for his sons, committing them to God's mercies, not only for the long road trip before them but also for the unknown future ahead of them.

Everyone waved as the old car rumbled out of the driveway and headed east. Ken looked back with sadness and joy. He knew his life would never be the same again.

He felt forlorn to leave behind the fun and freedom of his high school days and the security of his wonderful home. But as the miles rolled on, Ken began to realize that change in life was inevitable and that each of us is essentially alone with God in our own changing worlds.

As they drove on that day, the scenery changed. Their first night on the road was beneath a full moon and along the eerie landscape beside the mighty Columbia River. They rolled on through the plains of eastern Oregon.

Ken thought a lot about Margaret that night and was somehow comforted that she was seeing the same moon and thinking about him. That was his hope, anyway. He missed her, but a thought kept nagging at him. It was something his father had told him a few weeks before their journey started.

"You know, Ken," he said, "I know that you and Margaret. . ." His words trailed off. Ken and his father seldom spoke of such things.

Mr. Taylor cleared his throat and tried again: "Most people wind up marrying a college schoolmate. High school friends. . .well, they are seldom seen again."

The journey to Wheaton seemed to stretch on for days and days and days.

Finally, the dusty car entered the outskirts of the small town of Wheaton, population about seven thousand. It was too late in the day for the college offices to be open, so the group ate a few sandwiches and slept all night in woods bordering the highway.

In the dark, from the car radio came the strains of a popular song, "Everyone Loves My Margarita." Margaret was two thousand miles away at her home—having to postpone college for a year for financial reasons.

Ken was already homesick. He was physically exhausted, and his spirits drooped to a new low.

In the morning they drove to the campus and located the registrar's and dean's offices. They all enrolled and received their room assignments.

Doug, Ken, and their friend Bob found themselves a block away from campus at the home of the MacKenzies—an elderly, godly couple who treated their student renters as guests and friends. The two-dollar boarding rate was reduced because the three of them roomed together.

And so Ken's college years had officially begun.

FIVE

Ken's First Years at Wheaton

As he began his first year of college, Ken was surprised to learn of his own narrow view of the world. Some students spoke about how they had come so far west to attend school, while Ken had thought Wheaton was so far east. He had assumed, like many of his friends from home, that New York and Chicago were only a few hours apart.

He was also surprised that many of his new schoolmates had a devotion to Christ far deeper than his own. At home, Ken was one of the spiritual leaders of his youth group. Now he felt as if he were being challenged to go to spiritual depths that he knew little about—despite his godly background.

One aspect of his spiritual need was intensified at the college's annual autumn evangelistic meetings. Daily chapel times were lengthened, and a special speaker was hosted every evening.

Dr. Harry Ironside challenged Ken—and all the students—to live lives of commitment and integrity. Ken began to realize his need to commit his life to Christ with a new intensity. He needed to face his pride, lust, and all manner of other inward sins.

Ken found himself privately confessing his sins in prayer times and asking for God's help to remove them from his life. He did not feel an instant deliverance from them, but he was made freshly aware of these concerns of God regarding his life. He felt as if he had made a giant step forward.

Yet Ken harbored some elements in his life that may not have totally pleased God. He still had a goal in life to become rich and famous. He followed his brother's example and enrolled in a premed course of study. Doug planned to be a medical missionary—but Ken saw the practice of medicine as a likely path to becoming rich.

"Where are you heading, Ken?" Doug asked as he spotted Ken hurrying across campus.

"The student employment office," he replied.

Doug looked puzzled. "But you worked all summer."

Ken shrugged. "I know, but all of that—and all my childhood savings—won't cover all my costs here at Wheaton."

"They have jobs waiting for students?" Doug asked.

"They say they do. People who live around here call in and ask for students to work—cutting grass, putting up storm windows, doing odd jobs around their houses, mostly."

Doug followed him to the employment office and signed up as well.

But in 1934 the country was suffering from an economic depression, and the jobs were not as plentiful as they once had been. Ken managed to find a few hours of work each week, however, and he was grateful for any extra money he could raise.

Christmas vacation was approaching, and most students arranged trips home over the holidays.

Ken wrote in his diary, "I am so homesick this week. If I don't get home for Christmas, I think I'll just go nuts."

He carefully accounted for his finances. He added up all his savings and loose change and came up with a grand total of seventy-eight dollars that would have to last until the end of the year.

Going home would cost at least fifteen dollars. It was too much. Ken wondered if it would have been better for him to stay out of school for a year to earn more money.

That Christmas, Ken's parents sent him and Doug each five dollars. Even his old Sunday school teacher, Mr. Doty, sent a crisp one-dollar bill. Both Doug and Ken picked up as much work as possible that winter, and they ate cold meals in their rented room at the MacKenzies'. Fortunately, their aunt and grandmother lived in Chicago, and they spent a few days with them and had a few proper meals.

When they returned home to campus, they found a large box of goodies from their old Bible class—cake, cookies, cheese, jam, and candy. It was a touching gesture.

Margaret also sent cookies. She and Ken were writing to each other every other week, and if a letter was even a day late, Ken was well aware of it.

Ken joined the wrestling team in the 165-pound class.

He was not a standout athlete—but he did earn enough points to win a letter in his junior year.

Perhaps Ken learned more during his daily wrestling workouts than he did in class. Wrestling is an individual sport, a one-on-one competition, and it taught Ken about self-reliance and endurance in the face of painful weakness. He learned about the necessity of long hours of preparation for a few crisis minutes during the actual match. He was not sure how these skills and new awareness would come in handy for the future, but he was certain that they would be beneficial.

Ken's first year of college came to a close.

"What are you doing for the summer?" became a frequent question. Ken considered going back to the Oregon hayfields.

"Why not sell the Thompson Chain Reference Bible?" asked one classmate. "I did it last summer, and I made more money than you could working twice as long in an old hayfield. I made enough to cover my expenses for the entire year!"

"How do you get one of these jobs?" Ken asked, obviously interested. It might be his first step to getting rich!

"I can get you the name of the fellow I work for. But it's door-to-door work. You have to ring a lot of doorbells to make enough sales."

"Where did you work last summer?" Ken asked. "Around Chicago?"

"No. I got to work through North and South Carolina. It wasn't so hot there, and they covered my traveling expenses and everything. You ought to come to one of the meetings. They're organizing sales teams right now."

So Ken went to a meeting to learn more about the job. He was not intimidated by the long hours—twelve hours a day, six days a week. He worked that long baling hay.

The leader of the meeting told them how easy it was to sell the book. "Once you tell them that the Scofield Reference Bible is old-fashioned, out-of-date, and contains some sloppy theology, you've got a sale on your hands, for sure."

Ken was dumbfounded. Disparage the Scofield Bible? His father learned all his theology from that reference book!

Ken thought about that for a few days. Besides the disparaging remarks about a competitor's book, he was equally fearful about door-to-door selling. He had a timid spirit. It was a timidity that would plague him throughout his life—and prevent his bold witness when he had opportunities to share his faith. Ken was aware of his shortcomings in this area, and as much as he desired to change it, he found it most difficult to do so.

He turned down the job—and headed back to Oregon for the summer. There, he would also be able to see Margaret. Perhaps that was the most pressing reason for his decision.

Ken returned to the hayfields. His days were filled with hard work and long hours. During the weekends, he got together with old friends. During the week, he rubbed shoulders with a class of men he had previously known little about. Many of the workers were unmarried men in their thirties, and their Monday morning reports of their weekend escapades made Ken's hair stand on end. He was a preacher's kid, brought up with people who didn't do that sort of thing. He had been protected from knowing very much about unregenerate human nature. These fellows seemed to have no thought for anything but women, and no farmer's daughter was safe from their stares and vulgar comments.

Because of the long hours, one night Ken and the rest of the crew spent the night in a hayloft. The typical crude humor was persistent. One man kept everyone up with a long string of dirty stories and jokes.

"Knock it off," Ken called out. "It's late, and we all want to get some sleep."

His warning did nothing to stop the man's tales.

Exasperated, Ken called out again, "If you don't stop, I'm going to punch you."

The man kept on.

Ken, frustrated, went over to the man and punched his shoulder as hard as he could. That seemed to shock everyone—and the offensive fellow grew quiet and actually remained quiet for the rest of the night.

Ken knew that he had to remain above such coarse thoughts and speech. He realized that man's natural condition is a state of depravity and that exposure to the lusts of the flesh is extremely dangerous. Because of those early experiences, Ken began a lifelong aversion to pornography—in any and all its forms, including milder material available on television.

Ken realized that the men he worked with in the hayfields were just like him—except that God had been gracious to him and given him a Christian home and upbringing.

He fully realized the truth of the statement, "There, but for the grace of God, go I."

The final evening came before leaving for his second year of college. Ken walked over to Margaret's house. The two of them talked for hours on her front porch, amid the fireflies and crickets.

"Say, Margaret," Ken asked, late into the evening, "if I asked you to rate my personality, how would you rate it?"

She looked away for a moment and hesitated in her response. "You want me to be honest?"

Ken was surprised. "Of course I want you to be honest! Why else would I have asked the question?"

Margaret paused again. Ken was certain that her hesitation was not a good sign.

"I think you could do a lot of improving," she said, as if she had considered the question well in advance and was waiting for the right time to deliver her assessment. She went on to list a long series of his shortcomings.

Ken did not admit to her that he had expected her to reassure him rather than add to his list of worries.

The 1935 school year got off to a good start with the fall evangelistic services. The services were a great help to Ken's spiritual growth throughout all of his college years. Although the sermons were evangelistic, they were for Christians, too, as the speakers aimed to help the students grow in the grace of their Lord Jesus Christ. Many of the speakers appealed for the students to face themselves squarely and give up anything that was holding them back from God.

Ken wanted to be popular. In fact, he longed to be the

most popular fellow on campus. It was not that he wasn't popular—but he wanted more. During one meeting, the evangelist pleaded with the audience to yield themselves to God, and Ken struggled hard before he could say, finally, "All right, Lord, I commit to You this desire that I know is holding me back."

Ken admitted that the emotional high that came from his decision was partly psychological and partly spiritual—and the long-term result was cleansing. But the result did not come overnight.

SIX

Margaret

Ken's life throughout college consisted of mountain peaks of youthful confidence, independence, and comparative freedom, yet he was always aware of a personal valley—deep and constant.

That was Ken's relationship with Margaret.

Even though she was two thousand miles away, she was ever present with him. He wondered if she were making new friends. Were they Christians? He had no way of knowing for sure.

Ken admitted to himself that he was in love with Margaret, but he faced a monumental challenge. He was in love with her, all right, but he was not sure if she was the girl he should marry. Ken had an ideal woman in mind. His perfect mate would be a person with no peers, a woman whom everyone recognized as an angel. Anytime he was attracted to a girl on campus, he began to run a mental inventory, analyzing the girl's good points as compared to Margaret's.

One day Ken was busy moping about on campus.

A friend approached and said, "Hey, Taylor, you look like you've lost your best friend. What's the matter?"

Ken tried his best to explain. "I met this new girl last night, and she's a nice person. But then I started comparing her to Margaret."

"The girl you left behind?"

"Well. . .yes. And my thoughts are just in a whirl. This new girl has some excellent qualities—qualities that I think Margaret lacks."

His friend listened for a while as Ken described his perfect woman. Finally, exasperated, he said, "Look, Taylor, if you *could* find a perfect girl, she wouldn't marry *you*!"

But Ken kept looking. Occasionally he found a girl who rated higher on his points system—and then the fact that he loved Margaret threw him into another depression.

How could I abandon someone I love in favor of someone else even if she were more perfect? Ken wondered.

He walked back to class and prayed for the millionth time, *God, help me know what to do—to continue my relationship with Margaret or to develop a deep relationship with someone else on campus.*

There was no answer. There was no voice. There was no vision.

In desperation and disgust, Ken said to God, *My plight is like that hedge over there across the street—impenetrable. No way through. Look! I'll show You.*

And to demonstrate to God his impossible situation, he walked across the street to the hedge.

See, God, he explained, *I can't get through. I can't find the way. I am exhausted with trying.*

44

But just as Ken arrived at the hedge, he saw a hidden pathway through, where students had worn a shortcut—invisible until one was on the spot.

Ken walked through, silent before God. Yes, God would show him the way. But when? And meanwhile, what was he to do about social relationships at school?

The battle continued.

During the summer after his sophomore year, Ken's friendship with Margaret renewed. Late in the summer, he suggested that she transfer to Wheaton from Oregon State College, where she was majoring in home economics.

Margaret had begun to use lipstick and fingernail polish, and Ken feared that she was becoming "worldly." He imagined that the environment at Wheaton would help change her spiritually.

Margaret was reluctant at first. Wheaton did not offer a home economics degree, and she was hoping to go to China the next year as an exchange student. But she was in love with Ken, and she assumed that his suggestion indicated that he was finally becoming serious about their relationship.

Late that same summer, an event occurred that would shake Ken's life and affect him forever. The experience began with a book.

One Sunday afternoon, after church, Ken came upon a small book titled *Borden of Yale '09*. The book was about Bill Borden of the Yale University class of 1909. Ken began to read and grew fascinated by his story.

It was obvious that Borden had a great love for God

and his fellow human beings. Those were qualities that Ken wanted for his own life, so he eagerly read on, hoping to find the answer and follow his example.

Bill Borden came from a wealthy home—his father had left him a million dollars, worth far more in those days than today. But Borden did not cling to that money. He considered it a gift and gave away hundreds of thousands of dollars.

Ken was aghast. Since childhood, he had thought that being a millionaire was one of life's highest goals.

Borden was a spiritual giant in other ways, too. He frequently talked to his classmates about his faith in God. He told them God had a plan for their lives and was ready to forgive their sins.

Up until then, Ken may not have ever talked with an unbeliever about his faith. Yet here was Bill Borden, millionaire, preaching at a gospel mission to down-and-outers. Borden was also an athlete—a wrestler on the Yale team.

Ken read on. This millionaire, athlete, and spiritual giant was considering going to the mission field.

Ken grew uneasy. A missionary was something he would never be—not because he had prayed about it but because he didn't want to go. He did not want to give up the good things of life in America.

But Bill Borden did. After Yale, he attended Princeton Seminary and began to be concerned about Chinese Muslims. He was ordained by Moody Church, accepted by the China Inland Mission, and assigned to a province where there was a concentration of Muslims. Then Borden traveled to Egypt to learn the Arabic language.

Ken grew more uncomfortable as he read on about

Borden's life. What if God called *him* to be a missionary? Would he go?

The story went on. Borden got to Egypt—and then took ill.

Ken had read many stories of missionaries with wonderful healing miracles because they trusted in God.

Dear God, Ken prayed, *don't let him die.*

But Bill Borden did die, and Ken was overwhelmed with shock. Then a cold thought gripped him: *If that is the way God treats a man wholly devoted to Him, then I want no more of such a God.*

It was a terrible moment as Ken deliberately turned his back on God. It was as if he were stepping off a cliff and plunging to the rocks below.

At that moment, God showed His grace to Ken in a way that was almost beyond his ability to tell it. He reached out and grabbed Ken and pulled him back. He could not describe what happened, but he found himself on his knees in prayer. He was praying in deep contrition, *Lord, here is my life. Take it and use it in any way You want.*

Ken never turned back from that decision—a decision that completely changed his life's direction. It was a decision that made it possible for God to lead him onward in a "guided tour" for the rest of his life.

While certain spiritual matters had been resolved, Ken's emotional situation with Margaret was anything but settled.

At Ken's urging, she would attend Wheaton the next year. Ken responded to her decision with pleasure and concern. He realized that she was expecting the two of them would "go steady." But Ken was far from being ready for that.

It turned out to be a dreadful year for both of them. Margaret had left friends and family and found it difficult to make a place for herself on a new campus. She and Ken dated occasionally, but most of the time, he virtually ignored her. Their infrequent dates left them both depressed. They both realized that Ken had betrayed her by what amounted to false promises about his intentions.

SEVEN

The Accident

Ken carried a small canvas zipper bag and planned to hitchhike home for the summer. He hiked across town to Roosevelt Road, and within a few minutes, he had a ride going west.

Unfortunately, the farmer who picked him up was only going a few miles down the road. The next car that stopped was a shiny new Buick whose driver kept it at eighty miles an hour whenever possible.

The driver and his wife were heading out to Cheyenne, Wyoming, halfway to Oregon.

"You go to school in Wheaton?" they asked.

"Why, yes, I do," Ken replied.

"What about all those strange rules you have there?" the driver inquired.

Ken was puzzled. He didn't think the rules were all that strange. "Well, we don't smoke or drink. And we don't have dances or go to movies. And we don't play cards. And we have to go to chapel each week. But. . .we don't think the rules are strange."

Ken could see the driver smile in the rearview mirror.

"It sounds strange to us. We're Jewish, and I can't say that any of those rules would be accepted at a school we might attend. I take it everyone is a Christian there?"

Ken waited a moment to answer. He thought that this might be the first time he had ever talked to a Jewish person. He began to get nervous. He supposed he would have to "share his faith," and he was apprehensive. "Yes, I think everyone there is a Christian. That means they believe in Jesus. You know. . .accept His sacrifice on the cross and gain salvation. . . ." Ken got tongue-tied and didn't know what else to say.

The driver changed the subject, and secretly, Ken was relieved. He suspected that he had done his duty.

At the end of the day, they stopped at a tourist camp. Ken had anticipated hitchhiking throughout the night, but the driver's wife was surprised and shocked. She immediately offered to pay for his stay in one of the small cabins.

Ken accepted and once again was greatly surprised by their care and concern for a total stranger—and a Christian to boot.

Ken parted company with the Jewish couple in Cheyenne, and he decided to continue westward, even if it was dark.

He got one ride—for about thirty miles—and then found himself alone, in the dark, on a not-well-traveled stretch of highway. He walked a little way off the road, thinking that he might sleep for a while and be better rested in the morning when the traffic increased. He was cold, and mosquitoes swarmed about him. In the distance he heard the howl of a wolf or maybe a coyote.

He despaired and prayed aloud, "Dear Lord, help me. What shall I do?"

"I had never experienced such a thing before," Ken said later. "And I have never again experienced such a thing."

It was not a voice, but Ken felt such a strong urge to get back out on the road that it was irresistible. He jumped up, dusted himself off, and rushed back to the road. He thought surely God was speaking to him. There would be a car waiting for him.

But when he got to the road, there was nothing—only darkness and silence. Then Ken heard an engine! It came closer and closer. He waved as it went past, but it did not slow down a bit. He was crushed and disappointed.

But then another car approached. It sped past, too, but then slowed down and stopped. A door opened, and someone got out and shouted back, "Is that you, Taylor?"

The driver was Bob Harrah, a Wheaton College classmate, driving to Portland with three other students. They were too surprised to realize that a miracle had just occurred. Ken opened the back door and got in. A girl moved over to make room for him—it was Margaret. After their stormy year together at Wheaton, she was not at all pleased to see him.

Ken may have thought it was cold outside, but it was nothing compared to the chill in the backseat.

They continued driving that night, heading west. Soon

Ken fell asleep, along with several others in the car.

An hour or two later, everyone was jolted awake by a crash of metal against metal, as an oncoming car sideswiped theirs. Their car began to careen wildly as they skidded past telephone poles, missing one by inches. Ken stared in fear as the road in the headlights moved away from them, then back again, then away, as they skidded completely around several times. Margaret was screaming, and Ken took her in his arms, trying to protect her, even though he had no idea what the next few seconds might bring.

The car bounced once, crashed past the shoulder of the road, and then landed upright in a six-foot ditch.

They all climbed out, and they were all unhurt. A few of them raced back to the other car and found that, miraculously, none of its passengers were hurt, either.

The passengers of the other car were students from the University of Washington, heading east to Chicago. Apparently one or both of the drivers had gone to sleep, and the cars sideswiped each other at the midline, sending both spinning into the ditch, one on each side of the highway.

Ken's driving companions returned to the car, and they all thanked their guardian angels for watching over them that night.

Margaret and a few of the others continued their journey the next day by train. It did not leave until late in the afternoon, so Ken spent a few hours with Margaret before she left. It seemed as though they were once again comfortable with each other, and Margaret seemed to be relieved at putting her year at Wheaton behind her.

The summer of 1937 was like Ken's previous summers

at home. It was full of hard work in the hayfields, with occasional Saturday picnics and canoe trips. Ken and Margaret were on good terms that summer. She even talked about the possibility of coming east to Ken's graduation. She planned to get a job waiting tables at her dorm and save the money to pay for her train fare. Ken looked forward to this and to getting letters from her again.

All too soon, summer was over and Ken headed back to Wheaton. It was a good year for Ken, filled with debate team activities, social events, student politics, and even some studying.

While at school, Ken dated different girls, being careful not to be seen with any one girl too often. He enjoyed Margaret's letters. But in late March, there was a most enigmatic letter from her. She said that she wouldn't be coming to graduation after all and, further, not to expect any more letters. Period.

Ken wondered what in the world he had done. Or what she had done. She did not say that she had fallen in love with someone else, but Ken thought it might be the case. He was baffled. That she was not coming to graduation did not bother him—but not receiving letters from her sure did.

About that time, Ken also received some crushing news from an academic standpoint. All senior premed students had taken aptitude tests before applying to medical school, and the test results were back. The professor in charge sent notes to the other students, congratulating them on their success. But Ken's note simply read, "Come see me in my office."

Ken showed up at the appointed time.

"Mr. Taylor," the professor said gravely, "I wonder if you would not prefer to get a PhD and teach biology rather than be a doctor."

"What do you mean?" Ken asked, not at all sure of his intentions.

"You want me to be more direct?"

"Yes, of course," Ken said.

"You have failed the medical aptitude tests. No medical school would admit you with such a low grade."

"What?" Ken sputtered.

"Your brother passed. So did virtually all of the other premed students."

"I failed?" Ken asked again. "But I'm an honor student."

"You are a smart young man. But maybe this is for the best. If you're not meant to be a doctor. . ."

Ken walked out of the office shocked and disappointed—and a bit bewildered, as well.

It took a long time for Ken to see this as clear guidance from God—and what God wanted Ken's future to be. It was one of Ken's first lessons in trusting God when He closes a door to a personal desire. While God closed one door, Ken had no idea where another door might open.

After graduation, Ken returned once again to a summer in the hayfields. Margaret was not there; she was spending the summer in Texas with her sister. Ken tried to forget her, but with no real success. In fact, his mental whirl was all the greater—with college behind him and no coeds around to choose between.

Since his medical school plans had crashed, Ken tried to rebuild his future. He wondered if he should go back to school to get an advanced degree in zoology or biology. He was also interested in genetics. His father urged him to attend seminary. Ken considered journalism. Or perhaps he should forget all about that and go into business instead. . . .

Ken realized that he was fortunate to have the opportunity to choose a career—when so many others in the world barely had enough work to eke out a living. It did not occur to him until much later that God might actually lead him into dark, hard years rather than into bright ones. And either way, if God was in control, Ken's life would be equally within His full, loving plan for his life.

EIGHT

Engaged at Last

Ken was working into the early fall that year—having no need to rush back to college. One day, he was surprised to see a car pull up to the field in which he was working. Harry West, Margaret's father, got out of the car and made his way through the field in his business suit. He was concerned for Ken, not because of his involvement with Margaret but because it was characteristic of him to be concerned for others.

"Ken, I heard that you're looking for work," he said.

"I am, Mr. West," Ken replied.

"I'm looking for somebody to help in my company."

"What sort of work, Mr. West?"

"Selling refrigerators."

Ken gulped. He knew it would pay better than a farm job, but he was scared to death of selling. Yet it could be a good experience. "Okay, Mr. West, I'll do it. I'll let the people here know I'm leaving and report to work in two weeks."

Two weeks later, Ken reported to work, nervous and wearing the only suit he owned. Mr. West greeted him, introduced him to his sales manager, wished Ken luck, and retreated to his office.

The sales manager looked gruff. "Let's go outside," he said. "I need to talk to you."

Once outside, the sales manager turned to Ken, obviously perturbed. "Mr. West had no business in offering you a job. I have no need of an inexperienced salesman. I'm sorry, but you can't stay."

Ken might have argued, but he felt an overwhelming sense of utter relief at that moment. He never wanted to be a salesman.

Ken was now unemployed—as was his father. Mr. Taylor's work at Albany College had stopped while Ken was in high school. He was out of work for two years after that. He had worked for a time as a superintendent for the Union Gospel Mission—but that, too, had ended. Thus, finances had been very tight for the Taylors. Thankfully, a former parishioner had left them a thousand dollars in his will, but that had to stretch for a very long time.

Finally, Mr. Taylor received an opportunity to sell tea, coffee, and other household items door-to-door. It was not glamorous, but it would have provided a steady, reliable income. He also considered selling aluminum cookware by getting friends to host dinners cooked in the aluminum pots and pans. The "guaranteed" earnings would range from several hundred dollars to a thousand dollars a month. In those days, one hundred dollars a month was a good wage.

"Ken, which one would you take?" Mr. Taylor asked,

thinking that his college-educated son would have some sage advice.

"The aluminum cookware for sure," Ken replied. "The money sounds great."

A few weeks after his father began selling the aluminum pots and pans, Ken arrived home to find his mother in tears. She cried that she was almost out of money for food and household expenses. Her husband's efforts had failed to turn up a single sale and left their budget in shambles because of the cost of the elaborate food for the dinners.

Ken felt horrible. His advice had resulted in complete disaster for his parents. He did learn a lesson, though—to be cautious about giving advice and to be wary of advertising claims.

But Ken did not fully learn an even greater lesson— that the love of money is the root of all evil. His advice to his father had been based on his own values at the time. His philosophy was to take the easy money, not the hard, daily grind.

Over Christmas, Ken's old friend Bob Denney stopped by. Bob was attending Oregon State.

"You're still interested in Margaret West, right?"

Ken admitted that he was.

"You'd better get a move on and decide, if you haven't already. I see her all the time with the same fellow on campus, and I think it's serious."

Ken was not sure what to do about it.

"Why not take a couple of courses there?" Bob suggested. "You would be near her then."

Ken thought it was a great idea. "I would be near

her—and then I could decide whether to commit myself or get her out of my mind."

Ken registered for a zoology class in the spring, but after his first several days on campus, he still had not seen Margaret. Finally, he telephoned her and asked her for a date.

"It must be springtime again," she said testily. "Once a year you seem to be ready—and then after a few dates, you back off."

Ken began to protest.

Margaret stopped him. "No. I don't want a date. If you ever make up your mind, let me know."

Back home on spring break, Ken decided that he could wait no longer. He hiked through the woods and fields near his home. His thoughts were a jumble, and he talked to himself.

Do you love her?
I do.
Then why don't you ask her to marry you?
Because I might meet someone better.

He stood still for a moment. *Well, you have to decide.*

Hours later, he cried out to the Lord, *O God, I am so confused, and I can't put off the decision any longer. I will ask her tonight. O God, don't let us make a mistake. Please, God. . .please!*

Later that day, he confided to Doug, "I'm going to propose to Margaret tonight."

"Well, it's about time."

That evening, Ken set off for Margaret's house, full of purpose. But the proper words did not come easily.

"Can we start dating again?" he finally asked.

She took her time answering. "Not unless you have marriage in mind."

Ken felt his resolve start to fail.

"I'll—I'll have to think about it for a few days," Margaret finally said.

Two days later, they met again, and they agreed that dating, with serious intentions, was now the plan.

Later, they met on the campus of Oregon State. Ken could hold his racing thoughts no longer.

"I don't know how to say this, but will you marry me?"

After waiting for half a dozen years for that question, Margaret quickly responded, "Yes!"

They sealed the promise with their first kiss.

Almost immediately Ken lost interest in his graduate studies, dropped out of school, and returned home.

They agreed they would not tell their parents of their decision right away.

Some time later, a letter came to Ken from Stacy Woods, who was working with InterVarsity Christian Fellowship in Canada. Ken's college roommate had given him Ken's name. They were developing both a camping ministry and an outreach into public high schools.

They offered Ken a job paying fifty dollars a month, plus travel expenses.

Ken realized that if he took the job, he would have to defer his father's dream of seeing him in a seminary. But he quickly agreed that it would be a good way to get some practical experience.

Margaret graduated that spring. She won honors for having the highest grade point average of all the students in the school of home economics.

Before Ken left for his new job, he and Margaret decided they needed to tell both sets of parents about their engagement. Margaret insisted that Ken go through the protocol of asking her parents.

"But why can't we both tell them?" he asked.

"We could," she said, "but we might as well start off on the right foot with them."

Margaret's father thought marriage was a good idea, but he recommended that they delay it until Ken had a permanent job. Ken explained about his current situation.

Then Margaret's father dropped a bombshell: "Go and talk to my wife."

This scared Ken. Margaret's mother had never been overly friendly to Ken, and he was a bit afraid of her.

He found her in the garden. "Margaret and I are planning to get married," he stammered.

She fixed him with her stare. Then she coolly replied, "I'm sorry to hear that. Have you talked to my husband?"

Ken said that he had.

Later that evening, Ken's own father had a similar brusque comment. "If you love her enough to marry her, what are you doing at home tonight instead of being with her?"

Unfortunately, Ken's questions and doubts did not melt away. Years of indecision had worn ruts in his thought process, and the ecstasy that he should have felt was only partial. Fortunately, Margaret did not know he was still judging her and comparing her with everyone else.

When he left for Canada, Margaret had a loveliness and a glow in her eyes that thrilled him—but at the same time he was troubled by his own doubts.

NINE

InterVarsity Pioneer Camp

Ken's first assignment at the InterVarsity Pioneer Camp was to be a counselor to a cabin full of teenage boys. This was a challenge, as the camp was not very well managed.

Ken was, at best, a novice swimmer, and he was given the responsibility of teaching beginners. Some of the boys improved by experience, but Ken was sure it was not because of his expert instruction. One day, the father of one of the campers arrived to visit his son. The father grew angrier and angrier as he watched his son flounder about during swimming class.

"I had expected better results than what I'm seeing now," he all but shouted. "Especially considering the high fees I'm paying."

Ken tried to apologize. "I'll—I'll try to do better," he said.

The father walked away, shaking his head and muttering.

The best part of that camp, in Ken's mind, was the after-supper mail call. It was wonderful when one of Margaret's letters arrived. Ken would head to the dock, get a canoe, and paddle out to the center of the lake. There, he could be alone—and free from the mosquitoes. Ceremoniously, almost reverently, he would open the blue-green envelope, his heart beating fast. He loved her beautiful writing.

No question about it, he thought, *I'm in love*.

The summer of 1939 passed quickly, and fall came. Two new InterVarsity staff members joined them, and with their arrival, Ken hoped for some training in procedures and processes, but to no avail. None of the local staff had a clear idea of what to do, and no one further up seemed to have the time to tell them. They were given a list of high schools scattered over a hundred-mile area and told to visit the principals and ask to speak for thirty minutes in a school assembly. Following the assembly, they were to find a faculty sponsor and begin weekly Bible studies with interested students in one of the classrooms.

Fortunately, Ken found out that many of the principals were familiar with the annual routine and could tell him what was expected. They referred Ken and his coworkers to the faculty member who had been the sponsor for the previous year, or helped them find someone who might be interested.

Some of the school principals obviously had no interest in the InterVarsity speaker at all. Ken found one principal who told him quickly that a group could meet only if a faculty sponsor volunteered, but that Ken was forbidden to speak to any faculty members about it. The principal then escorted him out of the building and watched him as he left—as if making sure that he did not find a friendly faculty member in the parking lot.

After six months away, Ken returned home over Christmas. He and Margaret had a wonderful few evenings together during the holidays. Her Christmas present to Ken was a hand-knit red sweater, which became his favorite for many years.

Ken then headed back to Ontario—back to the grind of visiting schools, speaking at assemblies, teaching Bible classes, and doing his best to lead high school students into stable Christian lives.

At the time, Ken could not tell how much of the seed sown actually took root or nurtured young faith. But years later, Ken would run into people he had met and taught who credited his ministry in Canada for the growth and fruitfulness in their lives.

The following spring, Ken had the opportunity to head home for a short break. At the time, Margaret was working as a consumer representative for Northwestern Electric Company. They only had evenings together, so there was no round of parties as there had been the previous Christmas. And since the two of them were separated most of the time, Ken felt their engagement was falling flat.

Margaret was excited about their marriage and went on and on about what items she had been able to buy for when they set up housekeeping—like towels, sheets, a sewing machine, and tableware. But Ken didn't pay much attention to all that. He was not thinking about marriage in concrete terms. For him, marriage was a rosy glow in the future and not something to rush into.

Ken didn't talk about it much—and may not have been conscious of his feelings on the subject. In reality, he wasn't all that eager to get married. He held the immature opinion that the romantic excitement would probably only last a couple of years—and then. . .well, he didn't like to think about the "then."

Ken preferred to survive on the rosy glow of his romantic illusions a bit longer.

Soon it was time to head back to the summer camp in Quebec. A fellow staff member included the following dispatch in his report to headquarters. It related to an incident that happened that summer.

> *The younger campers were taken on an overnight hike on the longer, easier climb up the mountain. Unfortunately, a heavy rainstorm caught them in the early stages of the ascent, so they took refuge in a sugar camp. After supper, they continued with the climb until they were high in the mountains.*
>
> *That evening when they were having their campfire, Ken Taylor suddenly appeared. He had been left in charge of the whole camp when the camp director had gone to town to get supplies. With his characteristic diligence, Ken felt that he had to make sure of the campers' safety, in view of the storm that had passed through the area. He had scaled the face side of the mountain to reach the campers by the shortest route. When he discovered that all was well, he headed back down the mountain by the same route.*

Ken TAYLOR

*The concern Ken showed for the campers'
safety, inspiring him to come up by that treacher-
ous route by himself in the rain and return in the
dark, made a deep impression on the boys. Ken
Taylor was a real hero.*

TEN

Life Together

After spending the summer of 1940 at the InterVarsity camp in Quebec, Ken headed back to Oregon. He planned to stay only a few days before heading off to Dallas and the Dallas Theological Seminary. Because of his father's urgings, Ken had applied there and had been accepted. He had planned to spend ten days at home and then begin four years of seminary work.

Then he and Margaret would have their wedding.

Ken traveled first to Wheaton, where he joined an old friend, Tom Lindsay, and his wife, Barbara, who were driving to the West Coast. They, of course, asked why Ken and Margaret were not planning a wedding right away.

"We can't afford it," Ken said.

When they arrived in Oregon, Margaret joined them for dinner. It was obvious to Ken that Margaret was being unusually quiet. It came time for Ken to leave, and they went out on the porch.

"Didn't you get my letter?" Margaret asked.

"What letter?"

"The one I sent to you in Wheaton."

"No letter came. Was it something important?"

Margaret could hardly hold her enthusiasm. "Yes! I heard from Dr. Lincoln at the seminary. I have a job there! We can get married next week."

Married! *Next week?*

It was too late in the evening to discuss all the ramifications, and Ken—being typically silent—did not mention any of this to his parents.

If finances had been the barrier to their marriage after eighteen months of engagement, then the barrier was suddenly gone. They would have a combined income of one hundred dollars a month, and with care, they could make that stretch far enough.

Now Ken had to deal with the reality of being married in a few days—rather than a few years.

They were both twenty-three years old.

Margaret wanted a small wedding at home with relatives and close friends attending. Ken favored a bigger church wedding. But they only had a few days. How could all the arrangements be made in time?

Close friends Elaine McMinn and Don Mortimore were getting married in a week. All their friends and family would be in attendance. To upstage their wedding by having it a day early would not be fair. And they had to be on their way to Dallas by Friday night.

Margaret's small wedding seemed to be the only alternative.

But Elaine and her mother suggested a double wedding.

The next few days were a whirlwind of activity.

Margaret shopped at every store in town to find an end-of-the-season wedding dress. They got the license, telephoned relatives, bought wedding rings, ordered announcements, arranged for flowers, and did all the like.

On the day before the wedding, a small package arrived that Ken had been anxiously awaiting. It was an engagement ring that he had purchased in Canada. In the year and a half that they had been engaged, Margaret had never said anything about not having a ring. But Ken thought she should have one during the fours years he had planned to be at seminary.

Little did he dream it would arrive just in time for their wedding.

The evening of the wedding came with breathtaking speed. Ken packed his few belongings, and the family stood together at the front door of their home. Ken's father began to offer a final prayer. As he prayed, Ken felt his mother's hand over his own. He was surprised and a little embarrassed. Their family was not given to any outward expressions of love for one another, and he would later find that being brought up with so much repression of emotion had been poor preparation for marriage.

At the wedding, Margaret was radiant in her floor-length white chiffon dress with a short train.

Dr. Mitchell gave a brief homily, and Don and Elaine exchanged vows first. Then it was Ken and Margaret's turn.

Ken held Margaret's hand and said, "I, Kenneth, take thee, Margaret, to be my wedded wife, to have and to hold from this day forward. . . ."

Ken wondered if he really knew what he was promising. *How could anyone know?* he thought.

" 'Til death do us part."

It was over. He had no time to daydream or fantasize. They returned up the aisle, smiling self-consciously at friends and relatives.

They did not have time to participate in the wedding reception. The ceremony took place at eight o'clock, and their train to Dallas boarded in an hour and a half. Following the recessional, they said good-bye to Margaret's grandparents, aunts, and uncles. Margaret changed from her wedding dress to a new blue dress, and Ken returned the black shoes he had borrowed. Then they drove off to Union Station, only a few blocks away, followed by their parents, brothers, sisters, and closest friends.

The small group crowded around together. Ken was assailed with the same doubts and uncertainties. Had they made the right choice? Was Margaret the right one? Had they acted too impulsively?

Ken's agonizing thoughts must have shown on his face, because his uncle took him aside and said, "Marriage is wonderful, but you look as if you've lost your last friend. You're going to spoil everything for everybody. Now go back in there and smile."

Ken obeyed, even though his heart was still in turmoil. He wondered why Margaret's mother had not been happy with their engagement. He thought that perhaps she recognized that he was not certain of his own mind.

During the train ride to Dallas, Ken and Margaret made out a tentative budget based on their combined income of one hundred dollars a month. The first item, they both agreed, was their tithe—ten dollars. That was followed by rent, food, utilities, and books. They weren't sure whether any money would be left over for clothing. Fortunately, the seminary did not charge any tuition; they relied on gifts from friends of the school to cover faculty salaries.

Wedding gifts arrived throughout the fall, which Ken and Margaret both enjoyed opening. They received quite a few cash gifts, and they were careful not to spend any of that money, having no immediate needs. Margaret's foresight in having stocked up on essentials came in handy.

Grandmother Taylor sent them sets of crocheted doilies in assorted sizes. They were put away until someday in the future when they might acquire some fine china to go with them.

They never did get that fine china.

ELEVEN

Seminary Days

During seminary, Ken's part-time job with InterVarsity was similar to the one he had in Canada, but he was now working exclusively with colleges and universities. Ken found the work to be extremely difficult. In general, he found the atmosphere on college campuses to be antireligious. Many of the students who were Christians were strongly denominational and were not interested in meeting for Bible study with an interdenominational group. Ken found few students from nondenominational churches, and most of them seemed fearful of openly identifying themselves as Christians. His work was generally disappointing, though on occasion there were encouraging exceptions.

"I think I'm a large part of the problem," Ken confided to a friend. "I'm so timid about personal evangelism. I can't help but think I'm ineffective at giving these students the strong leadership they need to get started sharing their faith with others."

"Keep working at it," his friend advised. "You'll get better at it."

When summer came that first year, Margaret and Ken had to decide how to spend the summer vacation.

Ken was feeling a call to Christian journalism and felt that such a call would necessitate some specialized training in writing. At one point he considered quitting the seminary and going full-time to a university with a strong journalism school. But he remembered his father's words that a seminary background would be good for any career in the Christian environment.

Ken thought he might take some summer school journalism classes. But there was no money to spare. How would he manage that?

He came up with an almost unthinkable suggestion: Margaret could get summer work at InterVarsity's Pioneer Camp for Girls in Canada—just across the lake from where Ken had worked the previous summers. Ken would live in Chicago, get a part-time job, and attend summer school at Northwestern's Medill School of Journalism.

"But we'll be apart for the entire summer," Margaret said with sadness.

"I know it will be hard," Ken explained. "But I think it will be the only way."

And that is what they did.

Ken worked nights at a hospital, which provided room and board, and took courses at the university during the day. He was terribly lonely for Margaret the whole time.

Back on campus in the fall, Ken and Margaret moved into a studio apartment for married students. They had their own bathroom now, but the walls were so thin that everyone knew what their neighbors on each side were doing at all times. Ken was keenly aware of their lack of privacy.

World War II had begun that December. The draft started, and many young men signed up. Seminary students were deferred until graduation, when they would enter the service as chaplains. Some seminary students entered the service right then, but Ken, being married, thought it best to continue with his education.

In the middle of the year, he was offered the job of dining hall manager at the seminary. The job paid a small salary in addition to room and board. He quickly accepted. Margaret, with her training in foods and nutrition, made out the menus, and Ken did the purchasing. Fortunately, they had cooks on staff who needed little supervision.

At least the job was less stressful than Ken's Inter-Varsity ministry work—with the exception of the constant complaints from the students. No matter what food was prepared, some diners always complained.

Ken reminded himself that he was learning how to avoid a critical spirit—and that his job as a Christian would be best served by building up, not tearing down.

One spring afternoon in 1942, Margaret and Ken went out for a walk, but Margaret kept lagging behind.

"Don't walk so fast, Ken," she called out. "We can't keep up with you."

Ken slowly became aware of the import of what his wife had just said.

She was announcing that she was pregnant!

Ken was excited and as happy about the pregnancy

as Margaret was. They had not talked a lot about having a family—though Ken thought they may have two or three children. Margaret had grown up with the idea of having six.

That summer they went home to Oregon and lived with Margaret's parents. The shipyard in Portland was building freighters to get supplies overseas, so Ken was hired as a journeyman carpenter, with union dues automatically deducted from his pay. He jumped from making 30¢ an hour for his work in the hayfields to $1.10.

Everyone was happy, especially the shipyard owners, who worked on a cost-plus basis. This meant the more people they hired, whether needed or not, the more extra profit they received.

Margaret was in full blossom with her pregnancy and prettier than ever when they returned to Dallas in the fall. Early one morning in December, she wakened Ken, and at five o'clock in the morning they walked the four blocks to the hospital. After twenty-four hours of hard labor, Margaret gave birth to their first little daughter. She was named Rebecca. It was a happy day in the Taylor house!

They had some savings from Ken's shipyard work to pay for the hospital and doctor charges, and they dipped into their wedding gift funds to purchase a crib, playpen, buggy, and used washing machine.

TWELVE

Introduction to Missions

Ken realized his shortcomings in regard to personal witnessing for Christ. But he was also sincerely committed to trying to give the good news of God's love to those in darkness. One method he thought of while at the seminary was to mail tracts addressed to all the box holders on some of Dallas's rural mail routes. Margaret and Ken agreed to use part of their tithe to pay for the mailings and postage—and with each envelope, they enclosed a postage-free business reply card inviting those who received the tracts to ask for a free copy of the Gospel of John. They had been able to get free Gospels from a tract society, and they were gratified and encouraged as they received scores of responses. Some people replied that they had received Christ—and of course, Ken and Margaret prayed for them.

During Ken's seminary years, he began to be more serious about his prayer life. Their one-room apartment did not provide much privacy for prolonged personal prayer, so Ken began to take occasional prayer walks around their neighborhood. Since Dallas Seminary was in a residential area, the fields and woods where Ken would have preferred to walk were not available. He did not take these walks every day, but they were frequent enough to help him learn how wonderfully God answers prayer.

Prayer had always been an important part of Ken's life. He knew his parents prayed for all their sons even before they were born. Ken could clearly recall the family prayers they had every day, sometimes before breakfast and sometimes in the evening. The prayers were never rushed. Ken's father was serious about the importance of making sure his children grew up knowing God and becoming familiar with His Word. After Mr. Taylor had read and explained a scripture passage, they would get down on their knees beside their chairs, which had been set in a circle around the wood-burning kitchen stove, and each of them took turns praying aloud. Then he would conclude the session with a fervent and usually lengthy prayer. By example, he taught them to pray expecting God to answer.

Ken tried to pray every evening growing up, but years later he could not recall the specifics of his prayers. He admitted, "They were more of the 'God bless everybody' variety before I jumped into bed."

Ken's prayer walks in seminary were the beginning of what became a habit for him. After seminary, when he began his career, he realized that prayer and daily devotional time were of the utmost importance and that knowing God through these two means of grace was essential to his spiritual well-being. He began to arise at five in the morning rather than six to read his Bible and pray. He began to record what he had prayed for on index cards and checked them off as the answers came in.

Later in life, Ken said of his prayer experience, "One of the great things I have learned through the years is that a regular prayer and Bible reading time is not possible without a lot of determination and discipline. We can become absorbed in the newspaper or other mind-improving reading. After many years of ups and downs in my devotional life—of success mingled with failure—I realize there is no solution except to make a regular appointment with God and stick to it. This means doing more than my best—I must ask God to help me stay on a regular schedule. When I don't, I know that I have missed the greatest privilege and opportunity of that day. My own time with God is usually before breakfast, although sometimes I keep my appointment late at night or even during the night."

It was during Ken's seminary days that he became more and more interested in missionary work. He had never felt called to become a missionary, but he was intensely curious about the effect of missionaries. He began to read books about the idea of indigenous missionaries—missionaries who worked within their own culture. At the time, the common practice was for missionaries to become the pastors of "native" churches. Ken imagined that a better procedure might be for those churches to be self-supporting rather than having their expenses paid by mission societies.

The idea was for missionaries to work themselves out of a job and then move on to new territory, leaving behind a self-directed, self-supporting church whose members were not dependent on money from America or other outside countries.

It is common practice today—but then it was a new and unique approach.

The Christmas vacation of 1942 began within two days after Margaret came home from the hospital with baby Rebecca.

About that time, two fellow students approached Ken. "Hey, Ken, you're just the man we wanted to see."

"Why?" Ken asked.

"Over the Christmas break, we're all going to Mexico."

"Mexico? Why?"

"To study some indigenous mission projects—just like the kind you're always talking about. You want to join us?"

Ken did not hesitate. "Indigenous missions? Sure. Count me in."

He spent the rest of the day arranging for the wife of another student to come stay with Margaret. She was under doctor's orders to stay in bed for another week.

Margaret greeted Ken's news with silence.

It was much later that Ken realized how absolutely insensitive he had been to Margaret. He had paid no attention to her needs. His earliest days of parenting were marked by this obliviousness. Years later, he remarked how astounded he was at his own thoughtlessness.

"It was always a problem with me through the years," he later wrote, "to make good judgments about priorities. I am still not sure how to balance personal relationships with 'the Lord's work.' But I am certainly aware that in this one instance I made a significant error."

While in Mexico, the students spent days visiting different mission projects and churches, speaking to different missionaries. They saw evidence of real godliness in some of the Protestant missionary outposts and particularly in the growing Pentecostal movement. Ken was confused, as were some of his friends. The Pentecostal movement was still anathema to their fundamentalist seminary—as well as to Ken's home church and home training. Ken wondered if they were wrong in refusing fellowship with charismatic groups—especially when seeing their effectiveness at making the gospel known.

Ken was set on visiting Eglon Harris, who he had heard was trying to teach the "Christian nationals to run their own show." Harris lived several hours from where they were staying, involving a long night bus trip. Ken was concerned, especially since he did not speak Spanish.

Ken debated if he should make this long journey. His friends had advised against it. Then prayerfully, he did something that he wouldn't recommend for others: He opened the Bible at random and put his finger down on the page. Ken landed in 1 Kings 12 on the account of Solomon's son Rehoboam, who ignored the advice of his elders and followed the urgings of his friends, which caused Israel to rebel against him.

Taking this as God's direction to ignore the advice of his friends, Ken ran to the bus and spent the night traveling with crates of chickens and a live pig tied to one seat. He arrived and went to look for Mr. Harris. Mr. Harris's father had come to Mexico as a railroad engineer fifty years earlier and had begun a small Plymouth

Brethren meeting. Fifteen years before Ken arrived, that small group had blossomed into three hundred. Then a financial crisis hit the larger town, and the people headed back to smaller villages. Now groups were meeting in fifty-seven villages, with as many as two hundred people in each one, along with Sunday schools averaging one hundred students.

Mr. Harris printed 150,000 copies of a four-page gospel leaflet each month for distribution in Mexico and Central and South America. His devotion to Christ was genuine and heartwarming, and his example challenged Ken and made him think more seriously than he had before about whether God might want him and his family as missionaries. It was a sobering thought, and Ken was relieved to see that he was not automatically rejecting it—as he had always done before.

Ken was glad he had made the long and dusty trip.

He also met with Cameron Townsend, the founder of Wycliffe Bible Translators. They were working to put the Word of God into a native language. He expressed joy that he had fifty-one young people express an interest in helping him in his task.

Ken's third year of seminary drew to a close. He was still unsure of what path he should follow—to be the pastor of a church or a full-time Christian journalist.

That summer, Ken found work helping a friend edit and produce the first issues of a new magazine of the Child Evangelism Fellowship—a work that was beginning to spread nationwide.

Ken found the editing work challenging and rewarding. He helped with the design and worked with the printer. He was rewarded when he was finally able to hold the freshly printed magazine in his hands. He prayed that it would be of benefit to any reader.

Another magazine was starting at the same time called *HIS*, produced by the InterVarsity Christian Fellowship. The editor, Robert Walker, had done a great job in putting together articles that would be of interest to Christians on college campuses. There were articles on spiritual growth, encouragement in evangelism, and short stories with spiritual significance.

Ken thought the magazine was extremely well done, and he was delighted and overwhelmed when he received a letter inviting him to move to Chicago and succeed Walker as the editor of the magazine.

"I don't know what to do," he told Margaret. "The dining hall job gets us the best housing, and we've got lots of friends down here."

Margaret graciously pointed out that he had another year of seminary, but added softly that it was his decision to make. At the time, she was pregnant again.

Ken did not pray about it long. The opportunity seemed to be the chance of a lifetime. He took off to Chicago, leaving Margaret and Rebecca (Becky) behind, to look for a place to live.

A few weeks later, Ken sent Margaret an airline ticket—an event in itself, since neither of them had ever been on an airplane before. A neighbor drove him to Midway Airport on the south side of Chicago to pick her up, and Ken proudly displayed their new home to her.

But he was not prepared for her reaction.

She burst into tears.

Apartments were hard to find during the war, and the apartment building was old and dingy. Apparently Ken had paid little attention to the soot on the wall and the rusty springs and sagging beds.

Ken admitted that he had neglected to see it through his wife's eyes. She would be there all day while he was at school and work.

But they set to work scrubbing the walls and painting and made it look as homelike as possible.

While working on *HIS* magazine, Ken attended Northern Baptist Seminary to finish his degree. The thesis for his master's degree was entitled "Success Factors in Missions." It was an attempt to analyze why some overseas churches grow and some do not.

Ken admitted years later that if he were to write the thesis again, he would be much less sure of the answers— or even if any answers really exist. In some areas, the Pentecostal Church was the fastest growing. In other areas, mainline denominations were.

The only factor, Ken wrote much later, that is common to all church growth seems to be the providence of the Holy Spirit, and He goes wherever He wills. "Our calling, as I understand it, is just to be faithful in the proclamation of the gospel to the ends of the earth, regardless of whether or not we see a harvest."

THIRTEEN

A New Job and a Growing Family

Three days after Becky's first birthday, Ken and Margaret went back to the hospital for the birth of their second child. The baby was a boy, and they named him John.

Right from the beginning, little John had difficulties. He had colic and cried in pain after each feeding. Sometimes he became even more agitated, with his cries escalating into desperate screams. Nothing his parents did comforted him, nor could they find the source of his discomfort.

A friend who was a nurse visited one day. She immediately suspected that the baby had an inguinal hernia. Doctors confirmed her diagnosis, and the infant was fitted with a small truss to prevent further rupture. He still had colic, but he eventually outgrew that.

Ken and Margaret hoped that the hernia would heal by itself, but that did not happen. The only permanent solution was surgery, which was performed a few years later.

When the time for that surgery came, Ken received

an unexpected letter in the mail. It was a check for one hundred dollars to cover the medical needs. The funds came from their church, and it comforted Ken and Margaret to know that people were thinking about them and caring for their needs.

Ken's work as editor of *HIS* was pure joy and every bit as fulfilling as he thought it would be. Ken also had his first experience as a book publisher. He helped prepare the first book InterVarsity ever published—called *HYMNS*. The manuscript was sent to a music publishing house to be typeset and printed, and Ken was told that the book would be ready in eight months.

A few weeks before the book was scheduled to be finished, Ken advertised its availability on the delivery date. When the books did not arrive on that day, nor the next, Ken called to find out where they were. He was told that the work hadn't started yet, but the books were sure to be ready in another five months. It was a publishing truth that he would encounter many more times in his career.

Eventually the books arrived. That little hymnbook went into several printings and was used for a number of years.

Ken and Margaret spent the summer in Wheaton, outside Chicago and away from the dirt and grime. Because of the war, all housing stock was scarce. Homes seldom appeared in the "For Sale" or "For Rent" sections of the newspaper. The only way to find one was to get information in advance.

They had the use of a rental home that summer, but as the season neared an end, they had heard of no other homes for rent. Ken prayed fervently, but there was nothing. They had no idea where to turn next.

At the last moment, they received a call from a local pastor who was moving into a parsonage. His mother would be joining him, and her house would be available for rent.

"What a glorious answer to prayer!" Ken said.

The completely furnished house was directly across the street from the Wheaton College campus, a prime location for additional income by renting extra bedrooms to college students.

Moving day for the Taylors was simple. They owned two cribs, two high chairs, a playpen, a baby buggy, and their clothing.

They rented three of the four bedrooms to five college girls, and the Taylor family shared the other. Everyone shared the only bathroom in the house.

A small but important event occurred in 1944. It was an event that would have lasting ramifications.

The editor of *Power*, an adult Sunday school take-home paper, printed a note in one issue inviting writers and would-be writers to submit stories or articles for possible publication. Margaret and Ken read the note with interest.

"Maybe I'll write a story and send it in," Ken said.

Margaret smiled at him. "It's a lazy Sunday afternoon," she said. "Both the children are napping. Let's you and me both write a story and send them in. I'll get the paper and pencils."

Ken imagined the college audience who read the magazine he edited, and he tried to think of a theme that might be helpful to Christians their age. He started one and discarded the paper. He tried again and discarded that, too. Then he tried one more time and began writing about a Christian girl who fell in love with a fellow student who, though a good man, was not a Christian. Eventually her good sense and knowledge of biblical teaching prevailed, and she walked away from the romance. He called the story "Love Is a Dangerous Road."

Margaret's piece was on how Christians should be looking forward to the Lord's return. Both her article and Ken's were accepted and published.

His small story started Ken thinking about doing more writing.

During Ken's years of visiting Christian student groups on campuses, Ken had felt their need for a better understanding of the reasonableness of Christianity and the reasons many of their professors didn't believe in Christianity. Ken spent several days drafting and rewriting material for a small booklet titled *Is Christianity Credible?*

The booklet pointed out that both the atheist and the Christian came to logical conclusions, all depending on their suppositions. The atheist begins with the premise that there is no God. He doesn't come to that conclusion by proofs but begins with that conclusion and then decides that since there is no God, there can be no miracles or fulfilled prophecy, and conversion is only psychological. His position is all very logical but has nothing to do with knowing the truth of his assumptions.

The small booklet was printed by InterVarsity Press in 1946 and was well received on college campuses. The booklet has been in print for more than sixty years.

With college girls living in their home, Ken and Margaret's

social life picked up because there was never a shortage of babysitters. They made friends, attended events at the church, and went to concerts at the college.

But there was a problem on the horizon. Who would care for Becky and John when Margaret went to the hospital for the birth of their third child, due in January?

Margaret's mother would not be able to come. In the end, it was Ken's mother who made the trip from Oregon. They paid for her train ticket but did not have enough money to pay for a sleeping berth for her. She assured them that she did not mind sitting up in coach, as she would see more of the country that way, anyway.

Ken and Margaret had no telephone then. At that time, it was difficult to get a phone installed because of the shortages in materials caused by the war. So their elderly neighbors gave Ken a key to their house so they could go in and call the doctor when it was time for the baby to come.

In the middle of the night at the end of January 1945, Ken made the trek to the phone. He then called the assistant pastor of the church, who had volunteered to drive them to the hospital, day or night.

A few hours after checking in, Margaret gave birth to their second daughter, Martha.

Ken had met Clyde Dennis, a printer and publisher in Minneapolis who was offended by the cheap, one-color tracts that were commonly used at the time. He made a radical change and used good-quality paper with full-color illustrations. One day, Clyde shared with Ken his vision of translating his tracts into other languages for use overseas.

Clyde had recently moved his business to Chicago, and he asked Ken if he would be interested in joining his newly founded company, Good News Publishers.

Again, Ken struggled with his inability to make decisions. He wanted to stay with InterVarsity and its vital campus ministry, but he keenly felt the need overseas.

Ken prayed and prayed, and one evening he finally felt peace of mind about leaving the editorship of *HIS*.

When he told Margaret of the decision, she was quite willing. She would go along with Ken as long as the Lord was leading him, even if she was not actively involved in the decision.

Ken later wished he had talked things over with Margaret more often. "Her judgment is frequently better than mine," he said. "And she provides a different perspective."

Ken and Margaret found a home to rent in Lake Geneva, Wisconsin. It would take a ninety-minute train ride for him to get to work, but Ken was happy to have found lodging. The rent for the three-bedroom was eighty dollars—a steep price, since Ken's monthly salary was only three hundred dollars.

Another baby was due in October, and again Ken had arranged for his mother to come in from Oregon. But after her arrival, there was still no baby. One week went by, then another, and another. They discovered that both Margaret and the doctor had miscalculated and were a month off in the timing. Eventually a second son arrived, and they named him Peter.

Having been away from home for much longer than she expected, Ken's mother had to leave for Oregon almost immediately after Margaret returned home from the hospital. When Ken saw her off at the train station in Chicago, he had no idea it would be the last time he saw her.

Five months later, he learned of her death when a secretary brought him a telegram from his brother, Doug. His mother had died of a stroke.

Grief and regret overwhelmed Ken.

Happy childhood and teenage memories mingled with self-condemnation that Ken was not able to help his parents meet their financial needs. And what would his father do now? He would be all alone after thirty-three years of marriage.

Ken and Margaret had no extra money for the train fare to attend the funeral. Friends offered to lend it to Ken, but he was strongly opposed to going into debt, no matter how noble the reason. He still owed his parents money from his college education. How long, Ken wondered, had his mother gone without a new dress?

Ken told himself that going home would not help her. Ken did not truly understand then that funerals are for the survivors—to share their grief and recount their blessings.

Ken later realized that his decision not to go was a mistake. A neighbor of his parents helped him realize this when he reprimanded Ken for what he perceived as callousness.

FOURTEEN

Frustrations and Fear

Ken's work with Good News Publishing was challenging. He wondered how one could go about getting American tracts translated into African and European languages and then distributed overseas.

Despite the differences in culture and points of view between America and other cultures, Ken forged ahead. He wrote to missionaries, sent them copies of the tracts, and asked for their help with translation.

He received an immediate response, and many of the missionaries earnestly set to work on the project. Ken was chagrined to find out later, however, that many of these fine folks tackled the job with more zeal than ability. Their efforts at translating the small tracts often resulted in the copies being reduced to either incomprehensible language or a sort of pidgin English.

Over the months, Ken became gradually aware that his grand plan of translating American tracts was not working. He was unsure of what to do about it. As Ken faced this truth, Clyde Dennis found someone in Switzerland to start a missionary printing plant there. Many of Ken's duties were transferred to that location, leaving him without much to do.

Ken wondered what he should do. His situation was not getting any better. After several weeks of questioning the wisdom of staying, he finally decided that it would be best to resign.

Ken had a growing family and felt angry with God for leading him to leave his work at InterVarsity. He sulked in a spiritual sense. He told God that he wasn't even going to try to find other full-time Christian work. If that is what God wanted, he would need to see a bolt from the blue, for without guidance that dramatic, Ken said he would never again discern God's will.

So Ken tried to find work in the Wheaton area. The local cab company said he was overqualified, and no retail stores were hiring. Finally, Ken found a job nailing together chicken coops made from precut lumber. He defiantly told God that he was being mistreated.

After a few hours of work, the Lord graciously brought Ken to his senses, and he realized his foolishness in not trusting Him. Finally, Ken prayed that if God wanted him in carpentry work, or any other sort of secular work, it was His business to decide, not Ken's.

After less than a week on the chicken coop job, Margaret told Ken that an old friend from InterVarsity had called. He was now director of public relations at Moody Bible Institute in Chicago. He knew of Ken's need for a job and called to see if Ken would like to come for a job interview for an open position.

In spite of his determination to follow God's plan

only a few days earlier, Ken was hesitant to work at Moody. He was influenced during his time at Wheaton College, where most of the students had thought that Moody, being only a Bible school, was educationally inferior to a liberal arts institution. He also felt that some of its practices and rules were extreme.

So it was with reluctance that Ken went into Chicago on a Saturday afternoon to meet with the director of the Moody Literature Mission. J. D. Hall, the director, was looking for an understudy before retiring in a year. He explained that the department's main function was to mail thousands of sets of Christian books and Gospels of John to schoolrooms—especially in the South. County school superintendents would supply the list of schools. Thousands of children would be reached with the good news of Jesus.

Ken was fascinated by the description of the work and suddenly found himself fretting that he *wouldn't* get the job, instead of fearing that he would.

A few days later, to his delight and relief, they called to offer him the position.

But Ken's old weaknesses asserted themselves.

On his first day of work, as he headed for his new office, he found himself slipping into his familiar patterns of uncertainty. He hoped he wasn't making a disastrous mistake. What a way, he confessed much later in life, to begin what turned out to be sixteen of the happiest years of his life.

Housing remained a problem for Ken and Margaret. They had a rental home for the summer, but the owners would be back soon. They had no other prospects.

"Well, Margaret," Ken said, "we may have to consider more drastic measures."

"Such as. . . ?" she asked, hoping it might be a workable solution.

"Maybe you should go back to Oregon with the four children and live with your parents."

Margaret's face fell. Her disappointment was obvious. Ken was upset, as well—more with himself than anything. Had he brought Margaret from a stable and secure home to a life of rootlessness and uncertainty? Margaret had shed only a few tears through all of this so far. Ken saw her as the stronger one during this dark and difficult time.

About that time, an acquaintance offered them an "opportunity." He had purchased an old, run-down hotel at the edge of Winona Lake Conference Grounds near Warsaw, Indiana. It was a summer-only hotel—with no heat or insulation. The owner had blocked off a hallway and made a makeshift apartment out of four rooms. But they would have to buy a coal stove for heat, and Margaret would need to cook meals on a single electric plate.

They were desperate, so they took the "opportunity." Ken took the train to Chicago on Mondays, camped out in his office during the week, and returned home on Friday evenings.

Margaret seldom spoke of that year. It was extremely difficult for her. She was living in an isolated place, cold and drafty, with little contact with neighbors.

Ken did purchase a car at that time—a twenty-year-old Dodge for two hundred dollars. After seven years of marriage and four children, they finally had family transportation.

Winter was hard. The pipes froze, the plumber made numerous trips, and the children huddled around the coal stove for warmth.

They had no money for Christmas presents that year—but a friend sent winter clothes for the children. And even forty years after the fact, Margaret would still get teary-eyed when she recalled the box of crayons and coloring books that came from a neighbor back in Wheaton.

It was the middle of a frigid January, and their fifth child was due any day. Ken hurried from Chicago and arrived in the middle of the night at the small local hospital. Fathers were not permitted then to attend the birth, so Ken stayed outside the delivery room and paced.

The baby began to arrive, but the nurses would not help deliver the child—because the attending doctor had not yet arrived. The nurses demanded that Margaret wait for the doctor.

Ken argued that the child was ready to be born, but the nurses, who seemed to be afraid of the doctor, refused to let the delivery progress as normal. They called the doctor again, and thirty minutes later he arrived, grouchy and surly.

The doctor ignored Ken and went to Margaret's side. Within a minute, the baby girl came out—silent and discolored. The nurses frantically slapped at the infant, trying to start the breathing.

One of the nurses said in a panic, "Quick—get the oxygen!"

The doctor snapped back, "Fool! If it isn't breathing, what good would oxygen do?"

At this point, Ken slipped into a side room, got on his knees, and prayed, *Lord, if this child is ever going to need You in her entire life, it is right now. Please let her live, Lord. Still, Lord, if for some reason—perhaps because of something in her life that You don't want her to face, or if she would not receive the grace of Christ, or would abandon Him—then Your will be done. But please, Lord, let her live.*

Ken hurried back to the room. Just then the baby started to cry. A few moments later, Ken hurried back to the side room and thanked the Lord for His kindness. Baby Janet came into their lives as a special act of God.

FIFTEEN

A House of Their Own

Ken and Margaret stayed in the old hotel for nine months. That summer, they went back to Wheaton, into the same rental home as the previous summer.

Ken was not the only family man searching for affordable housing. World War II had ended, and hundreds of thousands of men left the service, started families, and began looking for houses.

Another couple in Ken and Margaret's church, Doug and Virginia Muir, shared their housing frustrations. They were living in a poorly insulated trailer with their two small children. The two couples began to look for housing that might accommodate both families, perhaps a duplex.

They found a large house facing the railroad tracks in Wheaton. It had been divided up, and five families were living there. But they were cautious about buying the house and did not want to sign any purchase agreement until all the renters had left.

Nonetheless, the summer was over, and the Taylors had to find a place to live.

Friends Ted and MaryLou Benson stepped in to help and offered their basement as temporary living quarters. Their house already held eight, and the Taylors added seven more to a home that had only one bathroom and no cooking facilities in the basement.

The house they were interested in was still occupied, and it appeared that the tenants were taking their time in leaving.

Another property that was reasonably priced came up for sale. The lot held two homes—a smaller, newer home and a larger farmhouse. But at the last moment, the Muirs ran into some financial problems, and all seemed to be lost. Margaret cried as they drove away from the failed closing. The strain of living in such tight quarters was obvious to everyone.

Margaret did what she had to do. She left her oldest daughter, who was now in first grade, with friends, packed up the rest of the children, and moved back to the hotel at Winona Lake.

Even in the midst of such hard times, God continued to work. The Muirs settled their financial problems, and once again, the property with the two houses was set for closing.

Ken recalls what a great day it was when they took possession of their home at 1515 East Forest Avenue during Thanksgiving week of 1948. The house was old and had many shortcomings, but it was a home they could call their own.

The house had no furnace—all the heat was supplied by a potbellied coal stove in the middle of the kitchen. The bedrooms were not heated, and the kitchen had no cupboards or counters. The house had no real foundation—just cement blocks set at the four corners. One side tilted so much that any spilt milk ran toward the lowest corner.

Mark was the first child born in the new home. He arrived in 1951 on a cold January night—with no doctor and no anesthetic.

After six years of coal heat, Ken spent a summer vacation digging out the crawl space to install a furnace that would hang between the floor joists. When Ken first lit it, the furnace nearly exploded. Ken had not read the instructions correctly.

Margaret was not happy with Ken's installing the furnace by himself. It was symptomatic of a growing tension between them. She was hurt by Ken's indifference to their need for a larger house, and he felt her exasperation. Ken always thought his ideas were better than Margaret's, and she quietly resented his arrogance.

There were never harsh words between them, but Ken became very defensive and easily offended by any critical remark Margaret made—even if her words were never intended to be critical.

Sometimes Ken would march off in moody silence for hours at a time. Often Margaret was unaware that she had offended him and was perplexed by his moodiness. He would often walk for hours, seething over her comment, until his anger was spent.

Ken knew that he had no right to be resentful and angry, but he didn't know what else to do. He knew the scripture that said, "Husbands, love your wives, and be not bitter against them" (Colossians 3:19 KJV). And he believed and practiced prayer—and was deeply branded by Paul's admonition that husbands treat their wives properly, "that your prayers be not hindered" (1 Peter 3:7 KJV).

One night, Ken took a long walk. He had resolved that this tension must not go on. He saw two ways to respond to Margaret's criticism. One was to regard any criticism from her as a fault of hers that he had to live with—because she was such a childish person. But he knew that was wrong and would not work.

The other solution was one he found hard to bear. That was to forgive Margaret for criticizing him. Ken rebelled against that. It was unfair, he thought. Why should he forgive her for hurting him? Sometimes the hurt was deep.

Finally, Ken realized that the situation must end. Margaret did not need to change—Ken did. He would have to take the lead by acknowledging her criticism as valid, then trying to learn from her criticism—while forgiving her for hurting him.

That night he returned home and said that she had been right and that he forgave her for hurting him. It was hard for Ken to do, but God helped him. The next time it happened, his anger flared—but he kept it inside. He acknowledged and forgave. It happened again, and he followed the same plan.

Not many days later, he realized that his anger was becoming less frequent.

Several weeks passed, and Margaret remarked to him, "You are different than the way you were."

God's grace had prevailed. Ken's spiritual battle of so many years was ended, and Satan, who had conquered for so many years, was himself conquered.

That summer, they converted the back porch into a dining room and converted the front porch into bedrooms for the three boys. However, the front door of the house now opened into Peter and Mark's bedroom. And since the porch was not heated, it was cold in the winter. They installed storm windows on the inside of the rooms, holding some of the cold at bay.

The make-do measures were Ken's idea, not Margaret's. She hoped that the appreciated value of the property and their equity in the home would provide enough for a down payment on a larger house. Ken thought they should get by with less-than-adequate housing and save any extra money for the children's college funds—and give more money to God's work.

On occasion, Ken would arrive home and find a Women's Missionary Fellowship meeting in their home. Rather than disrupt the meeting by walking through the living room to get to his "study"—a desk in the bedroom, Ken would sometimes climb the apple tree that overhung the back porch and crawl through an upstairs window.

As the Taylor family grew to ten children, the Muir family next door grew to five, and other families in the neighborhood had youngsters, too. The yard was often filled with laughter and fun as the children played baseball, hide-and-seek, kick-the-can, and Red Rover. Margaret's father, on one of his visits, hung a rope swing from a tree in the front yard—a yard that was always filled with activity.

As the children grew, the older ones became embarrassed about the condition of their home. Ken was not aware of it at the time, but he learned much later that they would ask their friends to drop them off at the end of their long driveway. And they never volunteered their home for church youth meetings.

In the family's Christmas letter of 1960, Ken wrote: "Housing: Uncertainty prevails. We are finding it very expensive to fix up this old one. We have just had the downstairs bath completely done over, put in a new rear entrance, converted the pantry into a coat closet, etc. A good bit of vacation time was spent jacking up the north side of the house. Many lessons in patience and piety."

SIXTEEN

Traveling the World

Ken's work at the Moody Bible Institute was fulfilling. He was excited to have a part in the system of distributing Christian books and Gospels of John to schoolchildren.

Every fall, Mr. Hall visited some of the schools where the Gospels and other books had been sent to see how effectively they were being used. Ken was invited to go along on Mr. Hall's last trip before he retired. They drove to Kentucky, Tennessee, and Alabama, visiting several schools each day. The reception they received from both students and teachers was heartwarming, especially at schools "in the rural," which Ken learned was a local saying meaning out in the country.

Sometimes "the rural" was hard to get to, especially in Alabama, where they had to drive on wet, slippery red clay or deep mud to reach some of the schools.

When they arrived at the schools, the children pulled out the Gospels from their desks and held them high. The best readers took turns enthusiastically reading passages from the storybooks. Then Mr. Hall or Ken would give a little talk encouraging the children to read their Gospels every day and to use the other books for book reports.

Not long after Ken assumed these responsibilities, Peter Gunther took a position at Moody and accompanied Ken on some of these trips through the South to visit schools.

"I wrote the local pastor we were coming," Ken said as they drove through Kentucky.

"Do you always do that?" Peter asked.

"Not always, but I thought I should this time. And the pastor wrote back saying that he would alert the teachers about our visit."

"So they could get ready?" Peter asked.

"Sort of," Ken answered. "He wrote and said that if the teachers know, they'll tell their students, and the children will tell their parents."

"And that's a good thing?"

Ken looked thoughtful for a moment. "The pastor said that a number of these folks who live up in the hills do bootlegging on the side."

"Moonshine?"

"That's what he said. They're also worried about the 'revenooer.' It would be best if they know we're coming so we don't surprise anyone."

There was no direct road to one isolated school. They had to leave the car and hike along a stream in the woods. Both men were alarmed when they passed a shack and saw a bearded, grim-faced mountain of a man watching them with a shotgun at his side.

"Hello there," Ken called. "We're just heading up to the school."

The man did not answer, and both Ken and Peter turned back many times until they were out of his view.

When the two of them broke into a clearing where they were to take the trail up the mountain to the one-room schoolhouse, the atmosphere changed remarkably. About twenty-five children—the entire enrollment of the school—were waiting for them on the path. Full of enthusiasm, they rushed ahead and behind and around Ken and Peter, all along the one-mile hike to the top of the hill. There, the teacher greeted them, all smiles. They had a wonderful time.

Afterwards, two or three of the older students were designated to escort them down the hill, where they bid them good-bye. They were happy and thrilled about their welcome—but also glad to be back to their car and on their way again.

Over the years, Ken also took along his sons John and Mark and daughter Cynthia on the trips. One thing that impressed them the most was staying in hotels. They were also exposed to a part of the country and a segment of American culture that they might have missed otherwise. And it was a good opportunity for Ken to get better acquainted with his children on a one-to-one basis.

One day a young student came into Ken's office and told him of his plan to go to Mexico during Christmas vacation and distribute Spanish Gospels of John. Ken arranged for Moody Literature Mission to sell him several thousand copies at a below-cost price.

The young man was George Verwer, and this was the beginning of Operation Mobilization, which now has two thousand young missionaries scattered around the world.

One of Ken's dreams at Moody was to expand the work of Moody Literature Mission, which was given the task of developing Christian books in third-world nations. Ken began to write to missionaries, asking them what sort of books they would like to see published in the languages of the areas where they worked. He also made contacts at home and abroad to find out which missions were already publishing and distributing Christian materials.

The letters Ken received back indicated that overseas Christian publishing was sparse and haphazard at best. So Ken began to travel overseas to meet the missionaries in person and seek those with special interest in translating, printing, and selling books in local languages. Ken's trips took him out of the country for five to six weeks at a time. He sought out the places where Moody's financial assistance might be the most effective.

His first trip was in 1949. Paper was still scarce following the war, and he was able to supply much-needed material to several Christian publishers in Germany, Italy, and Spain. On a later trip, he traveled to India and assisted publishers there.

One event that occurred on an overseas trip made a remarkable impression on Ken—and illustrated his lifelong sensitivity to the despair he encountered around the world. One morning as he was staying in a Tokyo hotel, he awakened to the sound of the clomping of wooden clogs below his window. Crowds of people surged past the hotel on their way to work. As Ken looked out over them, he realized that only 1 or 2 percent of them believed in Christ, and the rest were all lost. He found himself almost hating God, who had made them, and he cried out against Him. Ken recalled being at the edge of a spiritual cliff, where the slightest push could have toppled him into an abyss. He cried out to God for help and mercy, and in the end he grew quiet before His sovereignty, although hurting bitterly.

A few days later, Ken was with a friend in England, and the friend told him that during the previous week, he had felt a great concern to pray for Ken. It was more than a whisper—it was an urgent call. He mentioned the day and time. As Ken thought back and allowed for time zones, he realized that it was the exact time when, halfway around the world, he had been undergoing his time of despair and horror.

One of the benefits Ken gained from international travel was the opportunity to get acquainted with some of the finest people in the world: missionaries and their families and the leaders of the national churches. Ken has been surprised and pleased to learn, years after, that even casual conversations were helpful to missionaries with particular needs, often along spiritual lines.

Years after he stopped traveling for Moody, a young colleague of Ken's received a letter from his father, who served with Wycliffe Bible Translators in Guatemala. He wrote to his son: "If you should have the opportunity to tell Ken Taylor hello for us, that would be nice. I still remember how much we benefited from his talking to us at Ixmiquilpan in 1969."

Traveling overseas was not without its hardships. Many

times, Ken encountered disdain from denominational groups and other missionaries who looked down on Moody or thought that Moody was too fundamentalist. Many a church official turned a cold shoulder when Ken announced his place of employment.

Once when flying from Africa to Brazil, Ken's plane began its descent, and the attendant made the usual announcements. Ken assumed that they were being told to fasten their seat belts, but the message was entirely in Portuguese.

The plane landed, but the person Ken planned to meet was not at the airport. Ken made fruitless calls to locate him. Finally, someone at the airport knew enough English to tell him that the plane had landed at a different airport than the one scheduled. The passengers had been taken by bus to the original destination. No doubt that had been the flight attendant's message—one that Ken could not understand.

He rushed out of the now-deserted airport. All the buses were gone, but a taxi was there. The driver said there was a Holiday Inn only a few miles away and he could take Ken there.

The driver started out on a paved road but suddenly turned onto a rutted road through what appeared to be an endless field, lit by lights well off in the distance. Ken's heart sank, and his mind was flooded with all the stories he had heard about bodies found lying in deserted spots with all their belongings gone.

The driver knew little English, and Ken knew no Portuguese.

Ken kept repeating, "Holiday Inn, Holiday Inn."

The driver seemed to be nonchalantly reassuring him

that it was ahead of them. They bumped along the open field and finally came to a paved road.

Even after Ken was registered at the hotel and safely in bed, his heart palpitated during the night.

Ken later found out that his junior high school neighbor had been praying for him regularly while he was on the trip. He knew that the boy's prayers were answered and his guardian angels had been busy.

Later on, as the household finances improved, Ken was able to take each of his three youngest daughters on extended trips while they were in high school. They traveled to India to visit *The Living Bible* translators, to Africa to visit Ken's brother at his mission hospital in Zululand, and to Russia.

SEVENTEEN

Moody Press

One year after Ken started work with Moody, he was asked if he would like to become director of Moody Press, too, in addition to his duties with Moody Literature Distribution.

"I'm not sure," he replied. "I find what I'm doing fulfilling. And the literature distribution is useful. Maybe the work would suffer without my full-time attention."

Ken was given a capable assistant, and that gave him confidence. He accepted the offer and became head of both departments.

The first day on the job in the new office, Ken got down on both knees and committed the work to the Lord, both in its outreach and in its business affairs.

That started fourteen years of enthralling and absorbing work, trying to get Christian books published and distributed across the nation.

One of the first problems Ken faced as the new director

of Moody Press was a large stack of perhaps a hundred manuscripts piled high in a corner of his office. Former editors and staff had felt they should be published, but Moody did not have sufficient capital to carry out such an aggressive publication program.

Ken dutifully read through each one of the manuscripts. Some were good, and others were not suitable for Moody to publish. He found it very painful to notify many of those authors that they would not be able to go ahead with their original intentions. Naturally, Ken's decisions created a lot of disappointment and tension—along with visits from some authors to plead the cause of their manuscripts.

Early on, Ken took a stroll through a warehouse that was home to hundreds of thousands of dollars' worth of books.

"Are these books selling?" Ken asked. "We sure have a lot of certain titles."

"Well, no, they're not," was the reply. "Moody never had enough money to hire salesmen to visit the bookstores."

"How do you get them to the customers?" Ken asked.

"We do publish a catalog now and again. Any bookstore owner can order them from there."

Ken did not realize it at the time, but God was working on both sides of the problem. A company called VanKampen Press had just been organized and had salesmen but not very much product to sell. The solution to their problem—and to Ken's—was for them to buy books from Moody and have their salesmen sell them. The money that this project returned was enough to start publishing new titles.

In the early years at Moody, Ken saw that the Christian

bookstore industry was not in a very good situation. There was only a handful of stores—perhaps a tenth as many as today—and they were often in out-of-the-way places such as the basement or second floor of a church. Many of the stores were operated by people who had a heart for the ministry but very little business experience. Ken began to discuss with others what might be done to rectify the situation—and specifically, what Moody might do to strengthen this weak industry.

Ken thought that if the strong stores could be gathered with the weak stores, the strong stores might provide wise business counsel. But at the time, there was no such agency or organization in place.

Eventually Moody came to a solution that now seems obvious—a trade organization.

The American Booksellers Association was a trade organization for general bookstores. Why not have a Christian Booksellers Association? And just as the American Booksellers Association held an annual meeting to discuss ways and means of increasing their business, so could the Christian Booksellers Association.

Ken figured that the basement of Moody Church would be a good place for Christian publishers to set up their booths, and they could ask members of the church to entertain out-of-town bookstore managers in their homes.

Ken finally decided that the day had come to move the idea forward. He saw himself better at ideas than actions, so he passed some of the tasks on to an associate, Bill Moore—such as calling local stores and inviting their managers to lunch to discuss the idea of such an organization.

In a matter of a few weeks, Bill had met with a dozen store managers, and they had incorporated under the name of the Christian Booksellers Association (CBA) and set dates for their first annual convention.

Ken was all set to protest that the hotel and convention hall they had selected was too large, but it was too late to make any changes.

The first convention met with great response—and now the CBA is a giant organization with over three thousand member stores.

Ken began to learn more about human nature as he exercised his authority on the job. He was puzzled by the huge accumulation of manuscripts and correspondence on the desk of his editor-in-chief, Elizabeth Thompson. He wondered if she needed additional help, or perhaps some better methods of filing or procedures. Rather than sitting down with her and asking her, Ken got the key to her office, which she always kept locked, and went in one evening after work and rummaged about. When she found out about it (apparently someone had observed Ken entering), she was furious with him—and rightly so, he admitted.

Ken struggled with knowing that it is important to have the right ideas, but it is even more important to implement them with the cooperation of those involved.

Because of Ken's long-standing difficulty with Bible reading, he was pleased to have Moody Press republish *The New Testament in the Language of the People* by Charles B. Williams in 1952. The book had been published fifteen years earlier but had gone out of print. Ken learned of the availability of the book and visited Dr. Williams in his home in Florida. He was a warmhearted scholar and was pleased to have his translation back in print. The book was a best-seller for Moody for many years.

Ken served as director of both Moody Press and Moody Literature Mission until the end of 1961. He enjoyed his time there, but he was being prepared for a change. While on a trip overseas for Moody Literature Mission, he kept a diary that began with a backward look at some recent events in his life:

> *Concerning myself and Moody Press: For the past three or four summers, during vacation, I have prayed about whether this was the place for me to be. Each time the answer seemed to be, and was, "yes." Nevertheless, as a question of priority of time and opportunity and strategy, the question persisted. I was not questioning the enormous usefulness of the Moody Press output, but simply noting that other Christian publishers were also fully engaged, and the question of what still needed to be published was becoming very thought provoking. I came to the conclusion that although there were probably places of more usefulness, this work as director of Moody Press was my gift and my calling, and where I work in the Lord's vineyard is not determined by my own ideas of strategic importance, but by where God puts me. And I never failed to realize the joy and privilege of leading this mighty ministry, and to recognize*

its continuing usefulness and potential.

During November 1961, I read the Psalms with interest and value for the first time, until then having read with boredom and some cynicism about King David the psalm writer. Nevertheless, the Lord loved David—and the Lord loves me, too, despite faults. Anyway, I was struck by the promised blessings and assurances, which I was enabled to accept very personally. This prepared me spiritually for a sudden change in direction in God's guided tour of my life.

The sudden change occurred when Ken was asked to devote his full time to Moody Literature Mission. He packed up his office and moved to a smaller, cramped office on another floor and tried to find enough work to keep busy.

EIGHTEEN

Family Life

People often asked how Ken and Margaret could afford such a large family. He admits that they may have been poor in comparison to the standards of most of his friends, but they always had enough good, simple food on the table. Moody Bible Institute paid its employees once a month, and Margaret used careful management to make the money come out even with the month's expenses. Ken had one suit with two pairs of pants, and Margaret made the rounds of church and charity rummage sales for clothes for herself and the children. Neighbors and friends often gave them their children's outgrown clothing, too.

Ken's biggest problem was not keeping bread and butter on the table—he and Margaret scrimped and saved to accomplish that—but was realizing that he was not giving adequate time to his children. Each child had his or her individual needs, and he tried to accommodate those needs on a daily basis, but his efforts were inadequate at times, and he knew it.

Ken's normal workday at Moody did not allow him much time with the children. He would get up at five a.m. for a devotional time, leave the house at six thirty (before the children got up), and walk nearly a mile to the train station. He would return home at six o'clock in the evening. He was frustrated about finding time and ways to give individual attention to each child. His inability to do that proved to be a long-standing source of regret.

One child, once reaching adulthood, told her parents that when she was young, she often longed to talk to her mother or father about life at school and many other things, but they were usually too busy to provide undivided attention. She has gone on to forgive her parents, but it pained Ken to look back and recognize this failure with all of his children.

Ken insisted on one extravagant purchase for his family—a set of fifty children's classics, which all the children could read on their own. They could hardly afford the expenditure, but both Ken and Margaret wanted the children to read good books.

They also decided early in their marriage that they would not have a television set in their home. They have never owned one, even after they could have easily afforded it. Ken thought it was too difficult to raise the children with exposure to television's frequent depictions of immorality and violence.

Ken and Margaret wanted their children to learn the elements of business and the responsibility of earning and saving money. Margaret had read about a local family whose children had an egg route, so she helped Peter start one. Each week, Margaret drove out into the country to a chicken farm and bought eggs by the crate. The children put them into cartons and delivered them in their little red coaster wagon within the neighborhood. They soon developed regular customers and standing orders, and they delivered as many as sixty dozen eggs per week. Their customers were happy to have fresh eggs delivered to the door.

After Peter "graduated" from the egg route, the next six children in turn inherited it. The boys also had paper routes, and the girls sold homemade cookies.

In addition to providing for his children, Ken was also greatly concerned for their futures. He was determined that they should all have college educations. With a salary in the mid-1950s of four hundred dollars a month and college expenses of at least sixty thousand dollars looming ahead for his ten children, he could see no way that he could save enough to cover that cost. He knew that they would have to attend on scholarships or work their way through. He even admitted that they might have to borrow money to go to school—which greatly concerned him. He would have hated for them to start their adult lives with huge debts.

Instead of saving the entire amount, Ken wondered if the stock market might be an option. He had several hundred dollars, so he purchased some stocks. It was all very exciting to Ken. A stock-savvy friend lent him several stock advisory sheets. Every recommended stock was certain to shoot upward in price—or at least that is what Ken thought.

Ken prayed for wisdom, made his selections, called a

broker to execute the order—and watched with chagrin as his stocks began to fall in value. Every day he scanned the prices on the market report and became more and more depressed.

One stock did move upward. His spirits rose when the price rose and fell if the price fell. He realized that his emotional highs and lows hardly constituted a fitting way to live, but in order to meet college expenses, there was no other way.

While he was dabbling in the stock market, another friend introduced him to a missionary who had purchased several hundred acres of land in Brazil with the intention of planting coffee. Ken bought eighty acres and joined him in the venture. He knew nothing about raising coffee, but he was interested in the big profits that were sure to come. They waited years for the first crop, only to have it wiped out by a frost. Then a forest fire devastated the land nearby. There was also tension between the mission agency and the property owners in the area. Eventually Ken gave up on that dream and donated the land to the mission to avoid further expenses.

Another investment required only thirty dollars. A friend told him that he could make good money raising Christmas trees. So Ken bought hundreds of eight-inch Scotch pines. He had a one-acre lot behind the house, and he dug hundreds of holes for the trees. The whole family helped with planting and watering. Ken was confident that in a few years, he would have thousands of dollars for college.

But Ken never read about the logistics of raising Christmas trees. He did not know that they had to be trimmed yearly to produce the right shape. By the time he realized the trees were oddly shaped, it was too late to trim them. Another dream of quick wealth faded.

The curious thing about Ken's worries over his children's college expenses was that he did not really need to worry. God would provide.

When the Taylor family could no longer find vacation cottages large enough for them, they started camping. Ken purchased a large army tent that they all fit into. He also bought a Coleman stove and sleeping bags from an army surplus store. Their first year of camping, 1955, was with eight children. They stopped at various sites along Lake Michigan. Margaret was seven months pregnant at the time—and did the cooking and washing for the entire family. She never complained, even though it was not a restful time for her.

The family's first major trip with all ten children was a camping expedition to Colorado. Margaret had to hold the baby on her lap the whole trip. They developed a rotation system so that everyone got a turn by a window. Sometimes they noticed people counting them when they piled out of the car at a rest stop. Finally, one of the children made a sign they could hold up against the window. It read 12 OF US.

On his way home from a trip to Japan in 1957, Ken stopped in Oregon to see his father. He had been living alone in the family home for ten years since his wife's death. He had a standing invitation to live with Margaret and Ken and had been to visit several times, but he preferred to live in familiar surroundings within driving distance of old friends.

Ken had begun to hear from his father's neighbors that his father had lost his driving skills and had had several near misses on the highway. When Ken stopped to visit him on the way home from Japan, he found that his father's car had broken down, and he was isolated without transportation. Ken persuaded him to join the family in Wheaton, and he agreed. He was eighty-three at the time.

The house in Wheaton was more than full, but they added a new room in the back. Ken dug the trenches for the foundation by hand, and they installed a separate heater so his father could have the room as warm as he liked.

What surprised Ken was his own inability to adjust to his father's arrival. His father was a genial person who was always the conversational leader in social situations, both as a pastor and as a father. As a commuter, Ken had little time with his children, and he cherished the open conversation around the supper table at night. His father, however, tended to take over the table talk, asking Ken about his day at the office, or telling about the people he met on his daily walks. Ken did not know how to ask him to be quiet enough to let the children talk without being disrespectful, so he let the situation continue and bottled up his frustrations.

Ken's sensitivity grew as his father slipped into senility. He would often forget where he had hidden his wallet and think that one of the children or a thief had stolen it. They usually found it in a drawer in his room.

Ken knew he wasn't handling the situation with his father with a proper attitude, and he looked on that failure as a terrible spiritual defeat. He was not sure what to do about it.

One morning when Grandpa Taylor was eighty-four and had been with them for a year and a half, he was alone at the breakfast table after everyone had gone.

"Grandpa's asleep," said one of the preschool children to Margaret. With one glance, she knew otherwise.

Ken had despaired about his poor relationship with his much-loved father and despaired that his relationship with his own children might come to the same end. In the ensuing years, however, Ken was grateful that his good rapport among his children and their children remained—and that his failures were not reenacted in successive generations.

NINETEEN

A New Kind of Translation

Over the years, Ken and Margaret had read all the available books of Bible stories to their children again and again. Most were geared to three- and four-year-olds. Some were on the life of Christ, some on Old Testament heroes such as Joseph and Daniel. But Ken could never find a book that covered the entire Bible for very young children.

Finally, Ken thought about writing one himself. He experimented with the idea and wrote a few half-page stories that could match the pictures on the children's Sunday school papers. Ken would hold one or two of his children on his lap, show them the picture, read the story he had written, and then ask a few questions to see if his words had been understood. His children's response to his experiment was good.

Ken had handwritten the material, so he arranged with the typing pool at Moody Bible Institute to type as much as he had written.

But partway through the Bible, Ken became discouraged. He wondered if he should continue with the project.

A few days later, a young woman stopped Ken in the hallway at Moody. She was very enthusiastic about the work of typing Ken's book. That greatly encouraged Ken, and he decided to finish it.

The next day, Ken went to the typing pool to thank the young woman for her enthusiasm and encouragement. He didn't see her, so he asked the supervisor whether the person who typed his manuscript was away for the day.

The supervisor looked puzzled. "Katherine typed it," she said. "And she's right over there."

But the person the supervisor pointed to was not the person who had encouraged Ken the day before.

Ken described the woman he had spoken with.

"There's no one in the typing pool who looks like that," the supervisor said. "And they're all here now."

None of them was Ken's encourager.

Ken believed it was an angel God sent to tell him to continue.

Ken finished the book, and it was titled *The Bible in Pictures for Little Eyes*. It was published in 1956 and has since sold more than a million copies. It became a best-seller for Moody, and *Publishers Weekly* placed it as number thirty-four on its list of all-time-best-selling children's books. The book has been printed in fifty-four languages.

Before writing *The Bible in Pictures for Little Eyes*, Ken had already completed *Stories for the Children's Hour* and *Devotions for the Children's Hour*. Both of those books have wide distribution, the latter now having gone to print over a hundred times. Ken considered it a children's condensed version of Dr. Chafer's theology course that he had taken in seminary.

The stories in Ken's books were those told to his children while on Sunday afternoon walks in the fields behind their home in Wheaton. Some were based on his own childhood experiences, some on situations the children knew about in the neighborhood, and some on his own imagination.

Once at a CBA convention, a young woman approached Ken and said with a smile, "I hate you! Your *Stories for the Children's Hour* has been the favorite of each of my four children. I am so sick and tired of those stories—especially the one about Mr. Bert, the cat! Why don't you write something else for them?"

When the book *Devotions for the Children's Hour* was published in 1954, Ken read from it for evening devotions with his children. But even the author realized that it was not as beneficial as reading from the Bible itself. So the following year, when Becky and John were going on thirteen and twelve, Ken began to read from the New Testament Epistles. He knew it was time for them and for the younger children, as well, to study doctrine and how to live the Christian life.

But the transition from reading stories of the heroes of the faith in the Old Testament and the miracles of Jesus in the New Testament to reading Romans and Galatians in the King James Version was difficult. Ken found it hard to hold the children's attention even though he stopped reading after every few verses to explain the words or to ask a question.

Ken found the experience painful—a reliving of his own struggles with Bible reading. So he began to pray about the situation and tried to think of ways to make Bible reading more attractive. Some of his ideas were fanciful. What if the pages of the Bible were of different colors? What about putting a fragrance on the pages?

One Saturday in 1955, he sat at his desk and began to work on a storybook. He soon grew tired of the project and once again began to ponder the children's spiritual needs. He kept hearing his father's words: "Unless you fellows get into the Word of God and get it into your lives, you'll never amount to much as Christians."

Ken prayed, *Lord, how can our family devotions become more interesting and valuable to my children, and how can I learn to read the Bible with more interest myself?*

He thought first about summarizing each book but realized that it would not get people into the text of the Bible. Then he got an idea: Why not restate each verse to make it more understandable?

Ken did not cry out "Eureka!" but his heart and mind leaped up, and he wondered if that might be the answer he had been searching for all these years.

He decided to experiment.

That afternoon, Ken took out his King James Version Bible, several fresh sheets of paper, and a pencil. He opened the Bible at random and looked at 2 Timothy 2. He read the first several verses, thought about them, and carefully analyzed them word by word and phrase by phrase. Then he wrote down their meaning in everyday language.

For example, in the King James Version, 2 Timothy 2:4 reads, "No man that warreth entangleth himself with the affairs of this life; that he may please him who hath chosen him to be a soldier."

Ken rewrote this, "As Christ's soldier do not let yourself become tied up in worldly affairs, for then you cannot satisfy the one who has enlisted you in his army."

Ken went on that way through all the verses in the chapter. With great interest and satisfaction, he read what he had written. That night, after supper, Ken read it to the family, then asked the children some questions to see if they had understood the verses. Ken was elated to see that they were able to answer—they had understood. He followed up the discussion with how the Word applied to their lives at home and school.

Ken was so encouraged by his family's response that from time to time he prepared another chapter from the Epistles for family devotions. He received a positive response from his restating—while the King James Version seemed to baffle the children.

One night after Ken explained the meaning of one particular verse from the King James Version, Janet, who was about eight at the time, asked, "But, Daddy, if that's what it means, why doesn't it say so?"

Ken wondered if his idea was really and finally the answer to his prayers and his concern of so many years—for both the family and himself. Gradually, Ken sensed a deepening of the conviction that he ought to paraphrase all the Epistles.

But when could he do all this writing? He worked all day and had a large family at home at night. His answer was to do his writing while on the commuter train. He systematically worked on Romans as he rode. As the train swayed and bumped, Ken balanced the Bible on one knee and his paper on the other.

In the evenings, after the children were in bed or doing their homework, he would review what he had written on the train that day. He had copies of all the English Bible translations on his desk, plus Greek word studies and commentaries. He wanted to be sure of every nuance and meaning.

Within a year, Ken finished paraphrasing all the Epistles, and he was elated to finish the work. He had the manuscript typed up and titled it *Living Letters*. But before he sent it to any publisher, he decided to reread it one last time.

Ken was annoyed to find that the very first verse in the manuscript, Romans 1:1, needed a few words changed for greater clarity. And so did verse 2. Then, to his dismay, he could see verse after verse that needed changes.

It had been a year since he began his work, but the manuscript was far from being ready for publication. He was resigned to going through the manuscript again, even though the process would take another full year.

Finally, it was typed and ready to be sent out. But once again, Ken went through the same agonizing experience. He kept seeing verses that needed improvement. He began editing again, carefully, for a third time. Another year went by.

One evening when reading to the family from the latest revision, Ken was brought up short by one of his daughters.

"Dad, who are you writing this for?"

"For you and the rest of the family—and for other families," Ken replied.

"Well," she said, "I don't think it's for me or any other high school kids, because the language is insultingly simple."

As Ken looked it over from her point of view, he could see that she was correct. He wondered if this should be just for children or for the average *Reader's Digest* reader.

He began revising again. Perhaps he would do a children's version later.

It was no simple task to raise the reading level. It took another full year.

Finally, the manuscript was done. He read it over and was satisfied.

However, Ken still wanted Greek scholars to review the work—especially the passages where the original meaning was obscure.

Another year of work took place.

During the years 1955 through 1960, Ken wrote and rewrote the manuscript of *Living Letters*. It became his most precious possession. He even wondered what would happen if the house burned down while they were away. The unused chicken coop was a distance from the house—in case of a fire, it should be safe. So Ken took to hiding his manuscript in an old cupboard in the coop.

In all, Ken made six complete revisions of the manuscript over a period of five years, in addition to his first year's work. At last, he read the manuscript all the way through without finding need for improvement. On a scrap of paper he wrote, "Finished final revision of paraphrase, December 27, 1960, 3:30 p.m. with praise to the Lord."

Margaret found that scrap of paper years later. It was later framed and hung in Ken's study.

Now to get *Living Letters* published—that was Ken's quest. He originally considered Moody as the prime publishing candidate, but he wondered if some of the staff might react negatively to it. Many people were devoted to the King James Version, and a paraphrase might upset them. As director of Moody Press, Ken could have made the decision. The president of Moody told him it was his call to make.

After much thought and prayer, Ken decided that it would be better not to risk involving Moody, so he mailed the manuscript to the religious department of a well-known secular publisher. Ken was thrilled when they sent a letter of tentative acceptance. They would provide a final decision in a month.

But at the end of that month, they wrote of their decision not to publish the manuscript. Liberal theologians liked it, but the evangelical scholars on their board could not tolerate a paraphrase translation. They said any translation must be on a word-for-word basis rather than expressing the *meaning* of the Greek text.

Ken was discouraged but still hopeful. He sent it out again. It was declined. Again he sent it to another publisher, and they, too, passed.

This was a setback that he had not anticipated. His own enthusiasm had grown each time he revised the work.

It may not have been surprising, after all his years at Moody Press, that Ken's next thought was to publish the work himself. The big problem, however, was paying the printer. Ken had a big family, a small paycheck, and only a few hundred dollars in the bank. He had no collateral that a bank would loan money on.

Undaunted by these circumstances, Ken found out how much it would cost to have the book printed. He asked a friend, Paul Benson at Lithocolor Press, for a quote on two thousand copies.

A few days later, Paul came to Ken with the quote.

"I read the manuscript, Ken," Paul said.

"And?" Ken asked.

"I really liked it. I can't tell you how impressed I was with it. It's so easy to understand."

Ken was excited by his friend's enthusiasm.

"I think this will be a great book," Paul added. "And I know you don't have any extra money. Let me tell you what I can do—I'll print the two thousand copies, and you can pay me as you sell them. Okay?"

Ken quickly agreed.

Paul was certain that *Living Letters* should be printed now. He took the manuscript back with him and began the typesetting process.

TWENTY

Voice Problems

At the time Lithocolor Press started the typesetting process for *Living Letters*, Ken left for a four-month trip to Europe, the Middle East, and Africa. Before leaving, he told Margaret that she would have to do the proofreading in his absence.

"But, Ken," she protested, "I have never proofed anything in my life, much less an entire book!"

Ken thought for a moment, then said, "Nonsense. You'll do fine. You're smart and very detail-oriented."

"But, Ken," she continued, "I don't even know what sort of marks proofreaders use."

"I trust you," Ken assured her. "And any good dictionary has a whole list of the marks proofreaders use."

Margaret's letters to Ken on his trip were restrained. She was having to stay up until one or two in the morning to keep up with the daily batches of galley proofs—the typeset pages—coming from the printer. She had eight children still at home then—five in grade school, one in junior high, and two in high school. Her days were very full.

On his trip, Ken caught a cold on the plane traveling from New York to Glasgow, Scotland. He arrived with a fever and went to bed. He woke the next day, feeling better, but with no voice. His business appointments meant that he had to do some speaking, and he whispered his way through the day as best he could.

A few days later, his voice seemed to return. But a week into his trip, he was addressing a group of missionaries in Portugal, and ten minutes into his message, his voice simply failed. The laryngitis had returned. He could not continue and had to stop and sit down.

If Ken had had the opportunity to rest his voice, things might have turned out differently. But he had eleven weeks of travel ahead of him, and he kept going. His voice was a problem the whole time.

The highlight of the trip for Ken was finding a package waiting for him in Jerusalem. It contained the galley proofs for *Living Letters*. After years of work and countless revisions, to see the manuscript in type was a glorious feeling!

Ken left his hotel and walked across the valley to the Mount of Olives. With great excitement, he began to read the manuscript. He began to rejoice before the Lord. He was especially touched by Margaret's letter, which said in part, "I have learned so much from these pages. The words have helped me understand the scriptures so much better. I am sure that they will help others as well."

Up to this point, Ken had not heard much comment

from Margaret, one way or another, about his project. He had felt that she was ambivalent about the value of the manuscript—especially in light of how much time it had taken him away from his children.

After he finished reading, Ken sat looking across the city of Jerusalem and praying that God would use the work for His glory. The thought came to him, *I'm sitting in the very land where Jesus used the five loaves and two fish to feed five thousand people. I'm holding what will be two thousand copies of* Living Letters. *Lord. . .look at these books as two thousand loaves to feed Your people.*

He worked out some simple math. If five loaves fed five thousand people, how many people would two thousand feed? The answer: two million.

But that's too big of a dream. But yet. . .Lord, please allow that someday two million copies of this book may be in print.

Years later, while *Living Letters* was still printed as a separate volume, Ken realized that the number of copies had indeed reached two million. And the number of copies of *The Living Bible* has surpassed forty million.

Something else of great significance happened that evening. In Ken's small hotel room, he began to consider whether there might be other parts of the Bible that needed to be given a thought-for-thought translation. Up until this time, Ken had given no thought to going beyond the Epistles, which had always been the hardest part of the Bible for him to understand.

Ken didn't have much trouble with the Gospels. But he did find the Minor Prophets (called minor because of their length, not their level of importance) to be uninteresting, mostly because of the poetic style in which they were written. He wondered if it would be possible to rephrase them in a way to make reading easier.

As he read the galleys of *Living Letters*, he began to see a whole new vision of paraphrasing the Old Testament, too. That evening, he began experimenting with the book of Isaiah.

When Ken returned home, family and friends were shocked to hear his voice—or lack of it. He could only speak in a hoarse whisper. Speaking had become more and more difficult for him, and others were having a hard time understanding him.

In the following months, Ken tried every kind of remedy that anyone suggested—sprays, potent lozenges, chiropractic and osteopathic treatments, psychiatric consultations, and hypnotism. He attended healing services, and friends in different settings laid hands on him in prayer. He went to singing teachers and voice therapists, too.

After three years, he received treatment that involved injections in his neck. Some of his voice recovered—enough to get along. But for years, he turned down all invitations that involved speaking in front of an audience.

Ken later learned that others have the same affliction, known in medical terms as spasmodic dysphonia, which simply means that the vocal cords do not work in harmony.

Some people saw Ken's affliction as a blessing in disguise because it enabled him to concentrate on paraphrasing the rest of the Bible. It was an effort that took the following nine years. Ken continued to pray that his "blessing in disguise" might be removed after his work was complete.

It was not. An article in 1976 described his voice as "almost gone. It is barely a whisper now. Even through a microphone it sounds cracked and tired."

Margaret noticed a change in his personality because of the voice problem. Ken had gradually become quiet and retiring, where before he had been very vocal, sharp in repartee, and quick in making puns. Now, by the time he got up the nerve to make a comment in group conversation, the appropriate moment had passed.

Ken was frequently misunderstood, and he found that it was often easier to let the mistake stand than to go to the trouble to correct it. Ken was frustrated, especially when it was Margaret who was not understanding him.

In his later years, Ken's voice improved as he participated in an experimental program at the National Institutes of Health. He received injections of botulin toxin, which paralyzed the vocal cords on one side and resulted in a stronger voice. After a few months the treatment would wear off, and another would be needed.

TWENTY-ONE

Living Letters

A few days after Ken arrived home, he spoke to the printer, eager to know if copies of *Living Letters* would be ready in time for the CBA convention in July.

"Well, Ken," the printer said, "it may be awhile."

"Why?" Ken asked. "I thought we would be done now."

"The job took a bit longer than we expected," he answered. The printer looked a bit uncomfortable. "Some of your changes, Ken—none of the typesetters could read them. And Margaret made a lot more changes than we expected. She took out hundreds of commas and changed most of the semicolons to periods. Every change takes time."

Ken did not have the heart to complain to Margaret, because she was working for quality, not speed. In order to have books at the 1962 convention, held in Chicago, the printer agreed to prepare several hand-bound copies of the work.

Ken felt much more emotional holding a copy of *Living Letters* than he had with any of his other books. This was God's Word, but by His grace it was Ken's work, too. All his labor came flooding back. He recalled his frustrations with Bible reading and the long hours on the train and at his desk to get to this point.

Ken didn't know how to thank God properly, but he recalled the offerings of fire made by the people of Israel in the Old Testament. Then he thought of the pile of brush in his backyard waiting to be burned. When Ken lit the dry branches, he stood there in the presence of God with the first copy of *Living Letters*. He prayed again the prayer he prayed on the Mount of Olives—that God would use the little book mightily for His kingdom and His glory. Then he sank to his knees and gave thanks that the book was finished. When the fire was burning brightly, he took the precious copy and with great emotion threw it reverently in the midst of the flames as an offering of firstfruits to God. It was such a private act of worship that he told no one about it for nearly twenty-five years.

Every company needs a name, even a company with only one product. Ken had always been fascinated by the story of the sixteenth-century Englishman William Tyndale. Tyndale's goal was to translate the Bible into English, even though there was a death penalty for anyone who dared to do so. The church was afraid that people would read things in the Bible that might contradict church traditions. So Tyndale hid in Belgium as he worked on the book. He had it printed and smuggled copies into England—a Bible that the average person could read and understand.

Tyndale was rewarded by being burned at the stake for giving the Bible in English to the people of England.

Ken also had a dream of giving to America a Bible that was easy to understand. So it was easy for Ken to call his fledgling company Tyndale House Publishers.

Ken rented a ten-foot booth at the CBA convention and placed a half-dozen green-jacketed copies of his small book on the table.

In the past, Ken had enjoyed the action of the Moody Press booth. There, he met with booksellers from around the country and enjoyed hearing how grateful they were for his children's books and how well the books were selling.

But Ken was lonely sitting at his tiny little Tyndale House booth. Many booksellers stopped to chat, but because of his voice problems, Ken could barely talk with them.

No one seemed to notice the little sign in back that read TYNDALE HOUSE PUBLISHERS.

Ken was not a salesman by inclination, and only a few sympathetic friends ordered copies of *Living Letters*. He knew he would have to learn quickly how to be a better salesman. So he went into the aisle with a copy of the book and stopped people who were passing by, explaining that this was a new copy of the Epistles. Then he asked them to name a favorite verse and read it from *Living Letters*.

The plan worked. People were amazed and pleased by the way some of the profound passages from the apostle Paul's writings had turned from hard, rocky wilderness into milk and honey. Almost everyone he spoke to ordered a copy or two. Some even ordered five!

A friend of Ken's, Gordon Mitchell, who was a Canadian book distributor, agreed to distribute *Living Letters*. He ordered two hundred copies. During the convention, Ken sold more than eight hundred copies. He was immensely relieved that most of the printing bill could be paid when the books were shipped, and he felt encouraged that eventually the entire two thousand copies would be sold.

Margaret helped Ken by typing invoices and labels for orders and for complimentary copies. They typed up four-by-six index cards for each store that listed the invoice amount. That was their order entry system for the next three years. Ken kept the cards in his desk drawer with a rubber band around them. When the stack grew, they moved it to a shoebox.

They purchased mailing bags and boxes, and the children all pitched in to help, assembling orders and helping carry them to the post office.

Ken waited with great anticipation for the stores to sell the books they had ordered and to reorder more.

He waited. . .and waited. . .and waited.

Even the Moody bookstore had displayed five copies on a counter. Ken would look every day to see if the stack was reduced, but it took weeks and weeks for a single copy to sell.

Month after month passed, and no reorders arrived. Ken became discouraged. He thought that all the publishers who had turned down the original manuscript were right—the book appeared to be "dead in the water."

He began to wonder how to get rid of the rest of the books. He sent a copy to the American Bible Society to see if they would want them on a donated basis, but they declined, saying that they could use only "standard" translations.

Ken thought about sending them to missionaries, but he didn't have enough money for postage.

Then one evening he came home and found a letter from a bookstore that had ordered five copies at the convention. He tore the letter open. They reordered—a single copy.

It was faint encouragement, but that same week, Moody Bookstore sold the four copies that had been there for months. They reordered—as did four other stores. Gradually Ken's spirits lifted.

Ken decided to send a sample copy of *Living Letters* to each store that had not attended the convention and to each store that had attended but had not placed an order. He included a letter saying they could have the copy for free if they purchased five copies. Or they could buy the single copy for two dollars. Or they could return the book in the preaddressed stamped envelope that Ken included.

Many of the stores bought copies. The Christmas season, traditionally a heavy book-buying season, was approaching, and Ken was receiving orders for twenty-five to thirty copies a day! He wondered, *Should we invest in a new printing? Will the sales hold steady or fizzle after the holidays?*

Ken decided to print more copies. *But how many?*

At twenty copies a day, they could sell five thousand copies over the next ten months. Then something happened that helped him make the decision. He received an order for fifty copies from the Berean Bookstore in Bakersfield, California. It was the largest single order from a single store. Ken telephoned them and asked how they were selling so many. The manager said that one customer in particular was purchasing them to give away. "Our other customers. . .well, they just seem to really like it."

That's what Ken needed to hear. He placed an order for five thousand more books. The experience of the store in Bakersfield was duplicated in other parts of the country. Soon orders were coming in at the rate of a hundred copies a day!

The second printing quickly began to melt away.

TWENTY-TWO

Tyndale House Grows

Interest in *Living Letters* continued to pick up dramatically during the winter of 1962–1963. The second printing was gone in a few weeks, rather than the year that Ken had figured. He quickly ordered five thousand more in February, and additional printings followed in April and June.

One day that spring, a representative from Billy Graham's headquarters came to visit Ken in Chicago. He had incredibly exciting news. Billy Graham wanted to give a free copy of *Living Letters* to anyone in his television audience who asked for it.

"Would you be willing?" the representative asked.

"Would I? Nothing would please me more!" Ken exclaimed.

The whole idea behind the long translation process was that the new translation would reach out as widely as possible. *Here is a God-given opportunity*, Ken thought.

They estimated they would need fifty thousand copies.

There is an interesting story about God's guidance in connection with Billy Graham's decision to give away copies of *Living Letters*: About the time Ken first started his efforts at paraphrasing in the mid-1950s, he was returning from a Christian literature conference in Cuba. His seatmate was a businessman named Doug Judson. Ken spoke to Doug about Christ, and he showed Ken a tract someone had recently given him. He said that it had helped him understand Christ's claim on his life. Ken thought their conversation was encouraging, and he continued to keep in touch with Doug after the trip.

When *Living Letters* was off the press, Ken sent Doug a copy. Doug wrote back to say that it was terrific. Meanwhile, he had become associated with the Billy Graham Evangelistic Association, and he often served as Dr. Graham's personal assistant.

Doug was very enthusiastic about *Living Letters*, and he kept recommending it to Dr. Graham. When Dr. Graham was hospitalized for a time, he had a chance to read the book that Doug had recommended so highly. Dr. Graham thoroughly enjoyed it, and at Doug's urging, the team decided to give a free copy to anyone who wrote and asked for it.

The decision to use *Living Letters* as a television giveaway was a bold step. Dr. Graham had never given a book away before as a premium to viewers—it was a step of faith for them to do so with *Living Letters*.

They asked Ken how much of a royalty he would require. The answer came easily—none! But Dr. Graham insisted that there be some royalty, so they agreed on five cents a copy.

Ken attended the CBA convention that next summer and advertised that *Living Letters* was to be featured on a Billy Graham crusade as a giveaway. He expected bookstores to respond in kind and buy more copies.

Exactly the opposite happened. Most bookstore owners figured that if Dr. Graham was giving them away, why would anyone want to buy one? No one stocked up on the book.

That fall, Billy Graham began his giveaway program a few weeks after the fifty thousand books were printed.

One day, the telephone rang in Ken's office. It was a member of the Billy Graham organization.

"Ken, you know we said we would print fifty thousand copies. . ."

"Sure," Ken replied. "Are you having trouble?"

"Well, we don't know how to say this exactly. . . ."

Ken's heart sank. He thought they must have printed too many and were going to ask him to take them off their hands.

"Well, we didn't have enough, so we printed a few more."

"A few more?" Ken asked.

"Yes, about six hundred thousand copies. We never really technically asked for permission to do that. So. . .do you think it would be okay?"

Ken assured them that it was and was delighted to give his permission to have the extra copies printed.

Dr. Graham's offer literally sowed the nation with the paraphrased Epistles—but not to the saturation point.

Readers who were being helped wanted more copies. Friends who had not seen the telecast wanted copies.

Christian bookstores were besieged. The hardcover copies they had in stock were soon sold out. Many people wanted a cheaper, paperback edition. As a result, Tyndale House began ordering paperback copies by the tens of thousands.

It was at that time that Tyndale House Publishers hired its first non-family staff. Old friends Doug and Virginia Muir had moved back to Wheaton, and Virginia offered to help whenever the rush of orders got to be too much for the Taylors. Over the years, Virginia served as typist, as English stylist on *The Living Bible*, and as Ken's secretary. She then became Tyndale's first managing editor, then assistant editor-in-chief.

Ken now had a new concern. Should he leave Moody Bible Institute? He loved the work. Could he survive without its pleasant daily routine? Without his salary, could he support his family? What would happen if *Living Letters* suddenly stopped selling?

He prayed for guidance. He prayed and prayed. His boss suggested that he work on his translation for a few hours each day and still keep his job at Moody. He tried for a few weeks but felt guilty about his long absences from his office.

Finally, Ken made a decision. He officially left Moody Bible Institute in October 1963. He felt unsettled and unsure for several days after, but a few days later, he was near the Wheaton train station on an early morning errand. He stopped and watched the commuters as they piled aboard the train. He knew that they would work hard all day and return home exhausted. Ken knew then that he had made the right choice. He was thankful for his job at Moody, even though it required commuting, but he was glad those years were in the past.

From then on, Ken's days were different. He spent long hours shut away in his bedroom study. The work was intense, hour after hour, day after day, yet he could not recall ever being so energized. Nor did he ever come to the end of the day with a dread of what lay in store the following day. For the next several years, he found the work challenging as he translated verse after verse, working his way through large sections of the Bible. Often he stopped to pray, asking the Lord for understanding in restating a verse. He also searched commentaries to find meaning if it was unclear in the text.

It was a seemingly endless process—writing, crossing out, and rewriting.

To keep up with the flow of orders for *Living Letters*, Ken purchased an old garage for one hundred dollars from a defunct local railroad. He had it moved to his backyard. They built a packing table in it, and the shipping operation moved from the children's bedrooms to the garage.

Large delivery trucks would rumble down the residential street, looking for Tyndale House, and Ken would instruct them to back up behind the house. They had no forklift, and union rules would not let drivers unload, so Ken and his sons unloaded the cartons one at a time. When Ken or the boys were not home, Margaret was pressed into unloading duties.

Tyndale published its second book, a Spanish translation of David Wilkerson's exciting *The Cross and the*

Switchblade. They printed one hundred thousand copies.

After many months of intense work, Ken completed work on the Minor Prophets. He called the book, which included the New Testament book of Revelation, *Living Prophecies.* It arrived in the spring of 1965. When offering free copies to television viewers, Billy Graham said about the book, "One of the needs of the church today is for the prophets to thunder forth, 'Thus saith the Lord.' In reading *Living Prophecies* my own soul has been stirred, my mind challenged, my conscience convicted, and I have rededicated my life to Jesus Christ. It is my prayer that this book will have the same effect on you."

Within a year, a million copies of *Living Prophecies* were in print.

Tyndale House continued to grow, outgrowing its small office space. Margaret continued to do the accounting, banking, and payroll—all by hand. Eventually the company splurged and bought a used, hand-cranked adding machine.

The company began to broaden their publishing efforts to include general Christian books. In 1966 they published Dr. Tim LaHaye's *Spirit-Controlled Temperament.* Two years later they published his book *How to Be Happy Though Married.*

Ken had not originally planned to paraphrase the Gospels, thinking that they were straightforward and easy enough to understand—even in the language of the King James Version. But an encounter at the 1964 CBA convention changed his mind. A young couple asked him when the paraphrased Gospels would be out.

"I'm not working on them," Ken replied.

"But why?" they asked.

"They're easy enough to understand as they are," he countered.

The young man smiled and replied by quoting from John 3:8, "The wind bloweth where it listeth, and thou hearest the sound thereof, but canst not tell whence it cometh, and whither it goeth: so is every one that is born of the Spirit." Then he added, "Can't you make that more understandable?"

Ken thought about it and soon after decided that he would begin work on the Gospels, as well.

Many months later, the Billy Graham organization said that they would use *Living Gospels* if they could be done in a few weeks. Ken spent weeks on the final revisions, and it was published in 1966. Despite his thoughts that the Gospels might not need translation, the press ran overtime. Soon more than a million copies were in print.

The decision to proceed with paraphrasing the entire Bible seemed inevitable, and it brought Ken both joy and fear. He was joyful because as he worked, he felt that this was indeed God's call on his life. But he feared the years of intense labor that lay ahead.

And so he began.

One by one, new sections of the Bible were paraphrased and published. *Living Psalms and Proverbs with the Major Prophets* appeared in the spring of 1967—the early days of the Jesus movement. One leader of the movement said that in his opinion, *Living Psalms* was one of the chief sources of nurture within the movement.

In 1967 Tyndale House published *The Living New Testament* in response to a great many requests to have all the volumes in one book.

One by one, Ken paraphrased more sections of the Bible. He felt excited. It was wonderful and fresh to feed on God's Word every day. He knew he was being used by the Spirit of God to make a positive change in millions of lives, and so it could change the life of the church.

Tyndale House grew even more. In 1970 two products stood out. A staff member of Tyndale had made contact with Dr. James Kennedy of Coral Ridge Presbyterian Church in Fort Lauderdale, Florida. Dr. Kennedy had developed an evangelism program for teams in his church to use when visiting newcomers and in door-to-door evangelism. The step-by-step presentation began with two questions: "Have you come to a place in your spiritual life where you *know for certain* that if you were to die tonight, you would go to heaven?" Then, "Suppose that you were to die tonight and stand before God, and He were to say to you, 'Why should I let you into My heaven?' What would you say in reply?" Tyndale published the material Dr. Kennedy used in this program, and millions of people have used *Evangelism Explosion* in the ensuing years.

In the same year, Tyndale published a book called *Dare to Discipline* by an unknown child psychologist named Dr. James Dobson. It was the first of many best-selling books by Dr. Dobson.

Tyndale had taken off and was running. The company soon became well-known for having some of the industry's top-selling books.

TWENTY-THREE

The Living Bible

The preface to *Living History of Israel* was titled "At Last!" Ken went on to write, "This is the final volume in the *Living* series of paraphrased scriptures, and I thank God for allowing me to finish the project."

His work of many years was finished, and the question on his mind was whether to publish the seven sections of the paraphrase in one volume, perhaps calling it *The Living Bible.* He wondered whether enough people would purchase a copy of the one-volume book when they already owned the individual books. But many people had pressured Ken to go ahead with the one-volume project.

Tyndale scheduled the release of *The Living Bible* at the CBA convention in the summer of 1971. Most of the staff at Tyndale house favored an initial printing of one hundred thousand copies. Ken was stunned by their request, fearing that the company would be saddled with thousands of unsold books.

Meanwhile, Edythe Draper, the company's production manager, had begun—without Ken's knowledge—to negotiate with paper manufacturers and printers to be ready for reorders amounting to one million copies during the next six months. Ken later admitted that he was most grateful for her foresight.

The sales department blanketed the country with advance promotion of *The Living Bible*. Many people in the company were sure that it would be a runaway bestseller. By June, one month before the convention, they had prepublication orders for more than two hundred thousand copies.

The first thousand copies of the first printing were numbered and autographed. An especially gratifying promotional opportunity came in July when Ken presented copy number one of *The Living Bible* to Billy Graham at his crusade in Oakland, California. Ken sat in awe on the platform as he looked out at the thousands and thousands who had come to hear Dr. Graham deliver a simple message of God's grace. He was even more awestruck at the end of the service, when hundreds and hundreds of people came forward to the platform to make decisions for Christ.

Billy Graham's public endorsement of *Living Letters* and *The Living Bible*, when it was published as a single volume, made an enormous contribution to the wide acceptance the books received in those early years. Ken was always grateful that Dr. Graham saw their value so clearly, endorsed them so warmly, and distributed them so extensively.

Copy number two of the first print run went to Ken's wife, Margaret, in a more private ceremony. Numbers three through twelve went to their ten children.

With the family being such a major part of Ken's life, he found it hard to see his children leave the nest, one by one. And he was not prepared for the late 1960s and the early 1970s when the Baby Boom generation, born just after World War II, came of age and headed into the Vietnam War era with all of its turmoil. Many of the young people in those days were disgusted with their elders for getting them into a war. Public and personal rebellion swept the campuses and affected many young people. Ken's children were not unscathed by that unsettled era, and some of their marriages did not last. Ken had thought as his children were growing up that family devotions would be a stabilizing factor under every circumstance. That turned out not to be true, but God was very gracious in eventually bringing stability out of the turmoil in the lives of his children.

One night during those troubled years, Ken returned home from the airport at two a.m. after a business trip. He was in deep distress. He had been with one of his daughters for an evening meal in New York. Ken had observed her spiritual confusion, but he did not know how to help her. On the plane ride home, as he thought and prayed about her plight, Ken thought about several of his other children and their unhappiness—marital problems and antagonisms or indifference to the church or to the family. They were walking down dangerous roads. As Ken arrived home and entered the silent house, he cried silently, overwhelmed with helplessness.

Ken had tried so hard to help his children from their earliest years—but had failed. He sank to his knees once again, praying for his children and their particular situations one by one, just as he had so many times before. *O God, my God!* his heart cried. *What shall I do? What can I do? Will You not help them? Do You not care?*

Ken felt as if his prayers were bouncing off the ceiling. He heard no voice to encourage him. There was no dream to instruct him. As he stood in despair, he noticed two Bibles on the table, left there after a group Bible study Margaret had had that evening. In his anguish, he picked up one of the Bibles and opened it at random, praying for some word from God. The verse that he put his finger on said, "The Lord your God has blessed you."

It was tremendous encouragement to Ken, but he was still concerned.

"All right, Lord, thank You," he said. "But what about the children? Am I to be blessed with their suffering?"

Then in as much despair as ever, he picked up the other Bible and put his finger down. This verse said, "The children will return."

Ken fell to his knees before God in deep thanksgiving for this personal promise. He held God to it. One by one, his children have become settled in their faith or restored to their family, one of them after twenty-three years away.

After so much social turmoil in the 1960s and 1970s, many young people were turning to Christ for the answers they were so sincerely seeking. Many of them had been alienated from traditional churches and were being won and discipled by a new and informal kind of evangelism, some of it with a strong emphasis on the charismatic gifts of the Holy Spirit.

The Jesus People, as some of the groups called themselves, were a receptive audience for the fresh, up-to-date vocabulary and contemporary style of Ken's version of the Bible. God was doing a new thing through the youth of America, and *The Living Bible*'s way of expressing God's Word was on hand at just the right time.

Over the years, some have said that *The Living Bible* was the cause of the revival fires in those days. Ken never considered that as truth. Rather, he said, it was the oil from the Holy Spirit that helped make the fires burn brightly and brought millions to a fresh understanding of God and His plan for their lives.

The distributor of *The Living Bible* in Canada, Gordon Mitchell, was challenged early concerning the sales of the book. Gordon was given the goal of selling ten thousand copies before Christmas that first year, and he was astounded by the request. They had never sold a tenth of that quantity of any Bible in that time period.

But Gordon committed himself to the challenge, and he personally visited all the major bookstores in Canada, insisting that even the smallest of them take a hundred copies. By Christmas, all ten thousand were sold, and store managers were on the phone, desperate for additional copies.

Secular bookstores in America were also wildly enthusiastic about the sales. The explosion of sales of *The Living Bible* was unprecedented in religious publishing and nearly so in secular publishing, as well. On most of the best-seller lists, a book could make an appearance with the sale of a few hundred thousand copies. But *The Living Bible* soon moved into the millions of copies, capturing the attention and awe of the publishing and bookselling world. The result was that *Publishers Weekly* featured *The Living Bible* as the fastest-selling book in America during 1972 and 1973.

In Texas *The Living Bible* was on the local best-seller lists for months. A survey indicated that 50 percent of the homes in Dallas owned *Living* Bibles.

Ken was excited and exhilarated to see millions of copies of God's Word rolling into stores. He imagined that the result of this wave of Bibles was a new trend in Bible reading. Before long, many letters and telephone calls showed Ken that the lives of readers were being dramatically challenged to an extent that he had never imagined.

Ken had many interesting opportunities in connection with the promotion of *The Living Bible*. For instance, astronaut James B. Irwin of the *Apollo 15* crew made arrangements for Ken to visit Cape Kennedy and meet more than forty of his fellow astronauts. Ken gave each of them a copy of *The Living Bible*. Later Jim Irwin took leather-bound copies of *The Living Bible* to the heads of state of the USSR and other Communist countries.

Ken also visited with the cast of the Broadway musical *Godspell*. They greeted him warmly, and they graciously accepted copies of *The Living Bible*. Ken hoped and prayed that the truth and significance of the "godspell" (an old-fashioned word for "gospel") that the actors were portraying on stage would take root in each of their lives.

The staff at Tyndale had their share of amusing stories about those early years of distributing *The Living Bible*. One of their favorite letters came from a young reader who said, "My puppy pulled my *Living Bible* off the table and chewed it while we were sleeping. Can you take the cover off, run it through the machine again, and put a new cover on it?" Ken insisted that they send her a new Bible.

Once, at a literature conference at Wheaton College, Ken met another man named Kenneth Taylor. But under his name tag he had written, "Not *the* Ken Taylor." He told Ken that the real Ken Taylor had been a constant problem. "Sometimes," the man said, "when people ask me to autograph their *Living Bible*s, instead of going through the hassle of an explanation, I just sign them!"

The summer of 1974 brought about a large advertising campaign with television commercials aired on popular shows of the day. Tyndale House also ran full-page ads in many popular magazines. The World Home Bible League embarked on a distribution of *The Living New Testament* to hotel rooms. Their copies had colorful covers to attract readers, and they used the startling approach of labeling the New Testaments "Free! You may take this book when you leave the hotel. If you wish to do so, you may send us a dollar to help cover the cost." In 1974 alone, they distributed more than 1.25 million copies that way.

People often asked Ken if he ever expected *Living Letters* and later the complete *Living Bible* to be so widely accepted. His answer was always, "Yes and no."

He had prayed on the Mount of Olives, many years earlier, that he might be able to distribute two million copies of *Living Letters*. Ken admitted his faith was partial, yet God gave him the privilege of seeing that goal accomplished. His hopes and fears were expressed in a diary he kept—two months before the first modest printing of two thousand copies of *Living Letters*:

> *April 11, 1962* [three months before publication]
> *It seems like people don't enjoy the Epistles much; they find them hard going—hard to understand without digging through the wording. I hope the paraphrase will help them, at least as an introduction to what the Apostles were saying. How lives would be radically changed if people could read the Epistles with ease and understanding. Well, I fear this "apologia" is useless. Some will praise the Lord for blessings received and some will think a paraphrase foolish, unnecessary, etc.*
>
> *Every author has great hopes for his book, and I am the same. If it turns out to be a dud, I will know that here, as in other things, I sometimes react with a minority and that just because it has helped me, that doesn't mean others are helped. We shall soon see.*
>
> *May 8, 1962* [two months before publication]
> *I must add these thoughts of the future, as I have been reviewing them this morning.*
> *1. That I must continue to grow in grace as husband and father.*
> *2. That I must keep praying the* Living Letters *will help multitudes of people and that God will do a miracle of circulation for His own glory as His people understand what the Epistles are talking about, as I feel so many now don't. And that the unsaved will read Romans and Galatians as well as the Gospel*

of John. How clearly Paul brings out the way of salvation by faith, not works or law. Oh, that all the people could read and understand this, that they may sit down and read with understanding and great profit instead of fighting their way through the underbrush of verbiage. But it may be that I have not reached this goal, and God will gift others and qualify them better. Yet, even if this is but a link in the chain, it is worthwhile.

3. If it has wide distribution, probably an effort should be made to set up a not-for-profit corporation to own it, using the profits to start a Christian digest magazine.

October 14, 1963 [after about 75,000 copies were in print]

Regarding Living Letters, *I am praying for others to be roused up and gifted for paraphrasing in their own languages.*

I am praying that as we enter this new era of tremendous sales (even millions) God will guide all the way and that we will be pliable and completely at His mercy all the way. And that we will know how to pray and praise as we should, with no limitation on what God is willing to do, by our own inadequate praying.

TWENTY-FOUR

Living Bibles around the World

One day in the mid-1960s, a missionary from Bolivia said to Ken, almost wistfully, "I wish we had *Living Letters* in the Spanish language. My whole life has been changed since I began reading it in English. I struggled with my Bible reading for many years until someone gave me a copy of *Living Letters*. Suddenly the words from God became clear and plain to me. Scripture passages I had never understood came to life. How wonderful it would be if my people in Latin America could have the same experience."

Ken thought and prayed about this. *Living Letters* was changing lives all across America, but what about the billions of people in the world who could not read English?

Something very unexpected happened one morning after Ken began thinking about this situation. The strange event made Ken believe that God was going to use *Living Letters* in a special way in other languages. God gave Ken a vision—a real vision such as He gave to Isaiah and Ezekiel in Old Testament times.

This was a great surprise to Ken, for he was brought up in a Presbyterian home, and Presbyterians are not supposed to have visions. Moreover, Ken was educated at Dallas Theological Seminary, where he was taught that God does not speak in visions today. And all his life, he had belonged to churches that rejected the idea of visions.

Nonetheless, as Ken wakened on that particular morning, he lay in bed for a few moments before rising. He found himself walking through a wood. Suddenly, a furrow was there in the ground ahead of him, the fresh earth turned over by a plow. Curious, Ken followed the furrow, and soon a second furrow was beside the first, then another on the other side, so there were now three. But that was not all. More and more furrows were added to each side as he walked. As Ken came to the edge of the woods, he looked to the field beyond. He saw more and more furrows that spread out and covered the whole earth. Then the vision ended. Puzzled, he lay there trying to think of what this strange event could mean. Then he realized that God had shown him the future of *Living Letters*. It was His plan for readable versions of the Bible to cover the earth.

But Ken wondered how the world could be covered with *Living Letters* if fewer than one person in fifteen spoke English. This question led him to feel sure that *Living Letters* would be developed in all the major languages of the world. Africa came to his mind, then Japan, Russia, and many of the other lands he had visited.

Ken thought and prayed about this idea of translating *Living Letters* into other languages. He consulted an almanac that listed the major languages of the world and the number of native speakers. He discovered that some five thousand languages are spoken, but almost 90 percent of the world's population speaks in one hundred of those languages. Ken was enthused. A goal of one hundred translations of *Living Letters* was a practical goal.

One of his missionary friends from Latin America was visiting, and Ken shared the idea with him.

"Do you want me to try translating *Living Letters* into Spanish?" the friend asked.

"Dear brother," Ken replied, "if you do that, I will be eternally grateful." Ken was elated, and he prayed diligently as his friend began the translation process from English to Spanish.

Many months later, Ken's friend completed the task, and the manuscript for the Spanish edition of *Living Letters* arrived. Ken eagerly opened the package and wished he could read it to find out how well it read.

Ken sent copies to other missionary friends and native Spanish speakers, hoping to receive their enthusiastic responses. After a few weeks, they began to write him.

"It is a good translation," one man wrote, "but it does not have the vividness or the clarity of the English *Living Letters*."

Another said, "This work needs to be done by someone born and brought up in the Spanish language. Only such a person can truly speak and write emotive Spanish."

And so, with many apologies to his friend who had done the translating, Ken abandoned his idea, and his dream ended in failure. Translating *Living Letters* into other languages would not be possible unless the Lord laid His hand on a "native" writer to make the Word of God as alive in Spanish as in English. But if there were such a person somewhere in Latin America, Ken did not know how or where to find him or her.

Yet as the weeks went by, the dream and hope would not go away. In God's good time, a friend of Ken's who was born and raised in Cuba expressed his interest in the project.

"Yes, I think I can create a Spanish translation like *Living Letters*," he said when Ken spoke to him about trying out a few chapters in Spanish.

A few weeks later, a longer manuscript arrived. Ken sent it out for comments, and it received enthusiastic approval. Ken and Tyndale House were starting a worldwide ministry of new translations. A foundation was incorporated in 1968 with the name Living Letters Overseas.

Ken was always clear in his translation principles and processes. *The Living Bible* has never been translated directly into other languages. Rather, it is used as a model of readability and understandability. *The Living Bible* in English is a thought-for-thought paraphrase, not a word-for-word translation from the Greek and Hebrew. A translation of the English *Living Bible* into another language would run the risk of straying too far from the meaning of the original texts. Instead, Ken's goal in each language was to create a new thought-for-thought paraphrase that would be as fresh and readable in its language as *The Living Bible* is in English. The English *Living Bible* is the model, not the source.

From Ken's travels, he knew firsthand how much these new translations were needed. Though Bibles in the major languages of the world already existed, they were often very difficult to read. Many of them were translated by missionaries who did not know the native language very well, and in the hundreds of years since those translations were made, the languages had changed in many ways.

Not long after the publication of the Spanish New Testament, Ken was on a trip to Mexico with Bill Ackerman, the general director of World Home Bible League. They had been seeking approval to distribute this new, easy-to-read paraphrase. On the way home, Bill asked Ken, "Why not expect miracles? Why not ask God for distribution of five million copies of *The Living New Testament* in Spanish?"

Ken smiled in appreciation of Bill's enthusiasm, but he was hoping for a distribution of perhaps one hundred thousand copies.

But Bill would not be denied. "Let's ask for miracles," he kept saying.

Ken finally agreed to pray with him for this to happen. And it did.

One part of the miracle took place in Bolivia.

In 1974 World Home Bible League had arranged for Ken to meet with Bolivia's minister of education. Ken was supposed to be there for ten minutes—but the meeting stretched into an hour.

The minister started reading from the Spanish *Living New Testament*. He exclaimed, "It is so clear!" He ordered fourteen hundred copies to give to all the teachers of religion in the public school system.

Several months later, the minister called World Home

Bible League. "Can we have a million copies as the religion textbook for our schools?"

At a cost of $650,000, every schoolchild in Bolivia was given a Spanish *Living New Testament*, not only to study in school but also to have as a personal take-home copy for his or her family. It was a breakthrough and an answer to prayer. Most children in Bolivia owned no books—and most materials were mimeographed.

Evangelicals in Bolivia have claimed that this event was the turning point in their ministry. Until then, they had to be cautious about distributing the scriptures. Now everything had changed. And because of God's laws regarding reaping and sowing, a million copies of *The Living New Testament* cannot be sown without reaping a harvest for God.

Eventually the minister of education and the president of Brazil heard about what had happened in Bolivia. Knowing that the students in their country would benefit from the scriptures, they requested twenty-five million copies of the Portuguese *Living New Testament* for Brazil's high school students.

In 1971, with the completion of *The Living Bible* in English, the name Living Letters Overseas was changed to Living Bibles International (LBI). Ken was often asked how LBI's work related to Wycliffe Bible Translators. People wondered if there was any duplication or overlap. Ken always answered that there was not. Wycliffe translators often used the same principles of making thought-for-thought, easy-to-read translations, but they worked in languages that had never previously been reduced to writing. Translators under the LBI umbrella worked in major languages that in most cases already had Bibles. The problem was that these Bibles often were not easy to understand.

One *Living Bible* edition that has had very wide distribution is the Chinese. Ken learned that local pastors in Taiwan had said that initially ten thousand copies would be sufficient in the country for years. But the impact of the translation was so great that nearly two million copies were in circulation within the first two years after publication.

One of the exciting events in the translation program was the development of the Arabic *Living Bible*. The work was done in Beirut and Cairo. As bombs destroyed Beirut during their civil war, the LBI translation team kept steadily at their task. Once, the unfinished manuscript was kept safe by the hand of God and His angels when a bomb penetrated the walls of the room where the book was being worked on. The bomb failed to explode, and the manuscript and the translators were unharmed.

When the translation was finally completed, the question was how many to print. The traditional Arabic Bible was being distributed at the rate of less than five thousand copies a year. People figured that ten thousand copies of the new translation might easily last ten years. But a Christian leader wrote a long article in a widely read church magazine, telling everyone of his deep appreciation for the Arabic *Living New Testament*. "This recent interpretive translation as a whole is blameless," he wrote.

The publisher sold seven thousand copies at the Cairo Book Fair during the first week of publication and three hundred thousand during the first year. The book has been widely distributed through general bookstores as well as churches.

TWENTY-FIVE

Commendation and Criticism

Ken soon saw that God was abundantly answering his prayers for large numbers of people to be helped in their reading and understanding of the Bible. Letters began to pour in from readers of *The Living Bible,* saying that they, like Ken, had once found the Bible difficult to understand, but now God was speaking clearly through their daily reading of His Word as expressed in the paraphrase. Many readers shared that at last they were able to read the Bible with real interest. Testimonies about the impact of *The Living Bible* came from people of all ages, all levels of society, and all walks of life.

Hundreds of thousands of scripture-starved men, women, and youth were finally reading a Bible they could understand. It was as though a great vacuum in their hearts suddenly sucked in the Word of God, and it filled and satisfied their lives.

A businessman wrote enthusiastically, "*The Living Bible* is the greatest invention since the wheel."

A Bible study leader said, "I cried when I realized that I could finally understand the Bible."

A student at a Christian school said, "We meet in our dorm lounge every night, fifty or sixty of us, and listen while we take turns reading aloud from the letters of Paul. I don't think any of us ever realized before what it was all about. Thank God for *The Living Bible*."

One reader wrote, "Your *Living Bible* has become an intimate part of my life and is directly responsible for my spiritual growth over the past six years."

Another wrote, "Not long ago, you made *The Living Bible* available through the Campus Crusade for Christ for a very low price. The results at our church have been absolutely wonderful. The total impact has contributed as much as anything to the movement of evangelism and discipleship God has begun in our midst."

One of the testimonies that surprised Ken the most was from Dr. Jerry Falwell, chancellor of Liberty University and pastor of the Thomas Road Baptist Church in Lynchburg, Virginia. Falwell had never preached from any other version than the King James Version, so Ken assumed that he would not appreciate *The Living Bible*. But that was not the case. Dr. Falwell told Ken of the blessing it was in his home, where it was the preferred text for family devotions. "*The Living Bible* has ministered to me personally every morning for many years," he said. "There is no way I can measure the spiritual contribution of *The Living Bible* to my ministry."

Bill Bright, founder and president of Campus Crusade for Christ, wrote, "*The Living Bible* has made the holy, inspired, inerrant Word of God understandable to the twentieth century. I believe it is one of God's greatest gifts to our generation. I read and study it daily with great personal benefit and blessing."

On another occasion Bill Bright wrote, "I want to express to you personally my deep and profound gratitude for the contribution you have made to the spiritual lives of multitudes of people around the world."

Charles Swindoll, author of many life-changing books and pastor of the large First Evangelical Free Church of Fullerton, California, said, "I like *The Living Bible* because it's like a stream of sparkling water wandering across life's arid landscape: intriguing, refreshing, nourishing, comforting. My thirsty soul is often satisfied by the invigorating wellspring."

A brief sentence from a letter from a pastor says much: "*The Living Bible* is the simplest, most pleasant reading of the Bible in my experience, which goes back more than forty years."

A similar statement from another pastor said: "I have read the Bible through every year for the last forty-five years, but this year when I used *The Living Bible*, it is the first time I read it with interest."

While many Catholics welcomed *The Living Bible*, others held back, fearing the disapproval of their church. The solution was to find a Catholic bishop authorized to give the official imprimatur and *nihil obstat*, a Latin phrase that means, in essence, "Nothing in here is damaging to faith or morals." This took place, and then the Apocrypha was added—paraphrased by a Catholic priest. No changes were made to *The Living Bible* itself.

Publication of the Apocrypha brought some protests from the evangelical community. Ken replied that if the additional material would help Catholics accept *The Living Bible*, then it was good. Ken wanted them to have an alternative to reading (or not reading) from their old, difficult Catholic translation. The result of this decision was that Ken was thrilled to see wide acceptance of *The Catholic Living Bible* by many in the priesthood and in parochial education, as well as by Catholic laity.

While millions of people accepted *The Living Bible*, many did not. Ken had interesting experiences with scholars. Many of them thoughtlessly condemned *The Living Bible* without even reading it.

One man, the president of a large evangelical seminary, was very much opposed to *The Living Bible*. Ken had the opportunity to meet him one day—and found that his position on *The Living Bible* had changed dramatically. He told the following story: His teenage son had not been particularly interested in reading the Bible. One evening, his son didn't come down to dinner, and he went upstairs to investigate. He found his son absorbed deeply in reading *The Living Bible*. This experience alerted him to the fact that he ought not to condemn it without reading it. He began to read it himself and found that it was substantially accurate and very interesting.

Many scholars were divided over the issue of the accuracy of *The Living Bible*. There was agreement that it was without peer for private devotional and family reading, which was Ken's primary purpose for all his work. Many professors who at once criticized the syntax of the paraphrase told Ken later of the help it was to them in their own personal lives.

An Old Testament scholar and member of the

translation committee for Today's English Version noted in his review of *The Living Bible*, "Examination of *The Living Bible* indicates that it was based on an informed and scholarly examination of textual problems and is much more than a paraphrase of an earlier English edition. This is welcome news to the translator who may be consulting his work."

Another scholar declared, "A paraphrase is capable of far greater (not less) accuracy than a translation forced to be literal."

One scholar wrote, "There is no denying the fact that *The Living New Testament* is a faithful, clear, idiomatic, and expressive representation of the meaning of the original. But in many places it is so dominated by fixed theological presuppositions that it should not serve as a model for translators."

Meanwhile, a friendly reviewer said, "No doubt the scholars may curl their lips and say the translators took too many liberties, but no doubt the common people will read it gladly."

The negative comments about *The Living Bible* clearly reflected the strong, almost fanatical loyalty some Christians have to the King James Version. Ken learned that many of those readers thought that the King James Version is the original, inspired Word of God and that anything else is an untrustworthy counterfeit.

Yet people read *The Living Bible* with enthusiasm.

Many times as Ken traveled, he met men and women who came up to him and began to tell, with variations, what has become a wonderfully familiar story: "I can trace my conversion. . .my personal surrender to Christ. . .my love for God's Word. . .my call to Christian service. . .the mending of my broken home. . .a better relationship with my children or parents. . .to understanding the Bible for the first time through reading *The Living Bible*."

Whenever Ken received that sort of confirmation of his early hopes and dreams, he thanked God for His faithful blessings on the work He assigned him back in the 1950s.

Ken was asked many times how the high degree of interest in *The Living Bible* by millions of people affected his outlook on life—did it make him proud? His answer all along was that in all honesty, he did not think it did. From the beginning, Ken was clearly aware that God had chosen him from several billion people to do this work for Him, and day by day and sentence by sentence, the power came from above. Ken acknowledged that he had little to do with it except to sit there and write in the most understandable way he could, using the ability God had given him. Ken was grateful that he completely understood that God hates pride. He knew that God gives to some people the gift of preaching, to some hospitality, to some the ability to work in a factory, and to Ken Taylor the ability to paraphrase. Everyone is at the same level—God's servants, worthy of praise or blame depending on whether they properly use the abilities He has given them.

As time passed, and as *The Living Bible* took its place in the 1970s as the leading translation next to the King James Version, the letters of protest diminished and almost stopped. Nevertheless, Ken was concerned by the fact that some of the letters had made valid points. He wanted *The Living Bible* to be completely accurate. He began the slow and laborious task of working it over. In some ways it was as difficult and challenging as the original paraphrasing. Month after month, in all his spare moments, weekends and vacations, Ken labored to improve it.

He was working at this time only on the New Testament letters. But when those revisions were complete, it still needed more work. And when that revision was done, still more work lay ahead. Over a period of nine years, several revisions were completed, and at last the final product went to a group of Greek specialists who diligently compared it with the original *Living Bible* text. When they completed their work, Ken had more changes to make. In many instances they thought the original *Living Bible* was more accurate than his revisions.

Ken realized that many years of labor on revisions had been wasted.

Later on in his life, Ken would realize God's timing. God solved the problem in a fantastic way—and led Ken to understand why He hadn't stopped him nine years earlier.

TWENTY-SIX

Tyndale House Foundation

Back in 1963, when Billy Graham decided to give away copies of *Living Letters* to his television audience— free to anyone who wrote in to request a copy—Ken and the staff at the Billy Graham organization thought there might be fifty thousand people who would respond. Ken had been overwhelmed with joy that so many people would be reading God's Word in this easy-to-read format and knew that they would grow in the Lord as a result. This knowledge and joy were all the payment Ken wanted or needed, but the Graham organization felt that a royalty was necessary. They had agreed on five cents per copy as a royalty rate.

Ken had taken out a calculator to figure out the rates. Fifty thousand copies at five cents per copy would come to a royalty of twenty-five hundred dollars. That was an amazing amount to Ken. It was a time when he and Margaret had more children than salary.

Nevertheless, Ken had a strong conviction that the

ability to write *Living Letters* was a special gift from God, and because it was His Word, He should get all the royalties. Ken called an attorney friend for help to set up a foundation with a board of directors. The foundation would be responsible to give away the money from the royalties to qualified charitable causes. Ken called the new organization Tyndale House Foundation.

When the Graham Association used six hundred thousand copies instead of the expected fifty thousand, the foundation suddenly found itself with thirty thousand dollars—a vast sum of money at the time!

In addition, Tyndale House Publishers paid the foundation a royalty of seventy cents for every copy of *Living Letters* sold to stores. Two million copies were sold that way, and an amazing total of royalties was amassed.

The same system of paying royalties to God was used for all the books in the *Living* series and for the nearly forty million copies of *The Living Bible* that have been printed. The royalties are paid to the Tyndale House Foundation; from there they go to hundreds of Christian organizations all over the world.

Following the publication of the complete *Living Bible* in one volume in 1971, the royalties were huge—several million dollars each year. Selecting which worthy projects to give money to was an immense task. All the letters of request from hundreds of organizations came across Ken's desk. He was in a dilemma. How could he give them careful attention while being president of a fast-growing company, deciding which books to publish, and making long trips overseas to supervise the translation of Bibles in several dozen languages?

Ken knew he needed help. If he could turn over the responsibility of the foundation to someone else, it would lighten his load considerably. Ken could think of no one more qualified than his son Mark, who had grown up with the company and seen it in action since the beginning. Mark was about to graduate from Duke University.

Ken approached Mark for his help, but it was not an easy decision for Mark. He wanted to "make it" on his own, not be accused of taking an easy path that some might consider nepotism. But finally he agreed and became the executive director of Tyndale House Foundation.

After his graduation, Mark got married, and he and his wife, Carol, spent the summer in Africa investigating the worthiness and appropriateness of various mission projects that had applied to Tyndale House Foundation for funding.

More than fifty million dollars has now been released by the foundation and distributed by the board of directors. Not all of the grants have been specifically for evangelism. Many of them have been to assist in book publishing around the world, and some have been for social service work of various kinds, such as famine relief. In one case, the foundation donated one hundred thousand dollars for the purchase of an airplane to transport food from a port city in Africa to famine-stricken regions that could not be reached by overland transit.

Here are just a few of the grants that have been made over the years, selected at random:

- $30,000 to a training program for secondary school teachers in southern Sudan

- $5,000 for the publishing program of Africa Christian Press
- $9,000 for two literature distribution vans in the Philippines
- $1,000 for a food program in schools in East Africa
- $4,000 for equipment for a missionary printing plant in East Africa
- $750 for airfare for a man going as a technical specialist to assist missionaries in a building program
- $35,000 to help build a dormitory for Daystar Communications, a research and training center in Kenya
- $1,000 for a children's service mission in Africa
- $5,000 for a literacy program in the United States
- $11,000 for the purchase of a Land Rover for use by a leprosy mission in Nepal
- $10,000 for the American Scientific Affiliation to develop a program regarding science and Christian faith
- $250,000 to the Billy Graham Evangelistic Association
- $35,000 to cover the first year's cost of putting Dr. James Dobson's radio program *Focus on the Family* on the air. (What a giant tree sometimes grows from a small acorn when it is nourished by God and His gifted people!)
- $2,500 for Spanish evangelism in the Chicago area
- $19,000 for child evangelism work
- $100 for library books for a seminary overseas

TWENTY-SEVEN

Tithing and Hospitality

The Old Testament is quite clear that tithes were an obligation for God's people. Giving a tithe means giving 10 percent of one's income to the Lord's work. In addition to tithe, God's people gave freewill offerings—not required, but appreciated by the Lord.

In the New Testament, the principle is not so simple. Now we are not required to tithe, for it is not only 10 percent that belongs to the Lord. Everything we have and everything we are belongs to Him—our money, our time, our talents. How much are we to use for ourselves and our families, and how much should we give to the church and other Christian organizations? How much do we give individuals who are in need? Do we buy a new piece of furniture or send the five hundred dollars to a missionary? How large of a house do we buy? What kind of car should we buy? Should it be new or used? If we buy a smaller house or an older car, should we immediately give the difference to God's work?

These are questions that Ken Taylor struggled with all his life.

"What one person decides correctly," Ken said, "may not be what another person decides is right—though both of them may be operating within the will of God as He instructs them."

Ken always believed that a tithe of his gross income is a minimum. He would add thank-you gifts to the Lord as frequently as possible. Ken was brought up to be a tither, meaning that even as a child, at least 10 percent of all income from his paper route and odd jobs went to the church or other benevolent work.

Even in the grimmest years financially, as their family was growing, Margaret and Ken felt it was a privilege and an obligation to take 10 percent of their income, before taxes, "off the top" for benevolence.

Ken sometimes wondered if this was fair to his family, but his answer was always yes. Ken believed that they could thankfully commit the tithe to God, and He would see to it that their many needs were met. And that is indeed what happened.

Not all of Ken's *desires* were met, but they wouldn't have been met anyway, even if he had used the Lord's money for himself. And he would have had far less peace of mind, for it is people's desire and obligation to do their best to follow God's principles. The Bible says in Ephesians 5:10 to "find out what is pleasing to the Lord" (NLT). Giving is one of those ways to please God, and it gave Ken pleasure over the years, as well.

As Ken's salary increased over time and his children left the nest for their own homes, Ken and Margaret were able to give away 50 percent or more of their pretax income. In addition, Tyndale House Publishers gave away 10 percent of its pretax profits. But Ken was reminded that the Lord was just as pleased when they were unable to give so much. "The Lord appreciates the widow's mite as much or more than the large sums. We have had the joy of giving in each phase of our lives and have received our full share of joy in return."

Hospitality was another aspect of the Christian life the Taylors believed in. Margaret always enjoyed entertaining guests for dinner. A few weeks after she and Ken were married, they started inviting other seminary couples over—one couple at a time, which was all they had room for, and even then someone had to use the corner of the bed as a chair.

The Taylors made a special effort to have visiting missionaries from church come for a picnic or dinner. When out-of-town guests visited Ken in his office at Moody Press, he always felt free to invite them to dinner at home. He eventually learned that Margaret liked to have a few hours' notice if possible, but it wasn't always possible. Either way, she welcomed them warmly.

In 1966 Ken and Margaret were able to build a new home in the front yard of their old home in Wheaton. It was a complete turnaround as far as the children were concerned. No longer embarrassed by their old, dilapidated house, they now felt free to invite their friends in and sometimes had the whole youth group over for a meeting or a party.

In later years, the Taylors' house filled up with children and grandchildren, especially during holidays.

Sometimes guests would spend the entire week of Christmas with them.

Margaret kept a bulletin board in her kitchen with a list of friends and acquaintances they planned to have over for a meal. Margaret never felt the need to serve special meals to their guests—simple fare of soup and salad was common, but perhaps with her homemade pie as dessert!

TWENTY-EIGHT

Magazines, Racks of Books, and Church Bulletins

Not long after the publication of *Living Letters* in 1962, Margaret and Ken were having a picnic at a park in Wheaton, where they ran into old friends Ted and Jeanne Miller. Ted was an editor at Scripture Press, publishers of Sunday school curriculum. Ken and Ted talked about their mutual involvement in publishing.

"You know what?" Ken said. "One of the goals I still have is to start a magazine."

"What kind of magazine?" Ted asked.

"For years I thought that there would be a market for a magazine—just like *Reader's Digest*, except that it would use articles from all the Christian magazines."

Ted appeared to be shocked.

"What's the matter?" Ken asked.

"I can't believe it," Ted answered. "For years I have been thinking of exactly the same thing!"

"Well, Ted," Ken continued, "if I ever have enough

money to finance it, we'll start that magazine. You could be the editor."

The following spring, as Tyndale House published successive printings of *Living Letters*, there was more than enough profit left over. Ken called Ted and said that they could proceed with the magazine. Ted could continue to work at Scripture Press in the evenings and weekends so that he wouldn't have to risk his job in case it didn't work out.

They decided to call the magazine *The Christian Reader*. They would publish the magazine bimonthly and sell it through Christian bookstores. The stores would put a display near the cash register, where customers would see the magazine and pick up a copy to add to their purchases.

They rented a small booth at the CBA convention and proudly displayed the first issue, which contained sixteen articles. It was designed to appeal to a wide variety of readers, so they chose articles from periodicals such as *Christianity Today, Decision, Eternity, Alliance Witness, Sunday School Times*, and *Bibliotheca Sacra*.

At first they sold the magazine only to bookstores, but they gradually developed a list of individual subscribers. They soon reached a circulation of twenty thousand copies per issue. Ted and Ken were excited to think that many copies were going out regularly into homes, with surveys indicating that each copy was read by more than two people.

Ken had expected the circulation to continue to grow steadily, so he was discouraged when the number of copies seemed to hit a plateau. New subscribers just balanced out those who canceled. He longed for the magazine to bring spiritual growth and encouragement to many, many more readers.

One cold Sunday afternoon in January 1965, he felt so deeply troubled by this that he put on a heavy coat and went out to the garage where he could be alone and talk to God about it. He spent an hour with God, telling Him in detail all the reasons why he thought God should give them one hundred thousand subscribers within one year.

As usual, Ken was not aware of any direct reply, but he returned to the house, hopeful that God was listening sympathetically. Remembering the many miracles on behalf of *Living Letters*, he was encouraged to expect the same for *The Christian Reader*.

An hour later the phone rang.

The caller was Bob Hawkins, a bookstore owner in Portland, Oregon. He had expressed interest in the little magazine at the previous CBA convention and had ordered a few copies back then.

"How's it going, Bob?" Ken asked, expecting to hear some general shop talk.

But Bob had a more specific reason to call. "You know that little digest magazine you publish?" he asked. "Well, it's terrific, and it ought to have twice the circulation—and I know how to do it. Send me a thousand extra copies."

"A thousand? Are you sure?" Ken asked.

"I am indeed."

Two weeks later he called for another thousand.

"Bob, what are you doing with them?" Ken asked.

"I'll tell you later," he replied. "Let me test my idea a little more, and then I'll call you again."

In due time, Bob did call with his report. He had

given sample copies of *The Christian Reader* to local pastors. He urged them to take a regular supply of the magazines and encourage their congregation to pick up copies in the foyer after the service. The price at the time was thirty-five cents. The church would pay the store, and the store would then pay Tyndale House.

Ken thought the plan ingenious. They spent a lot of time revising the operation and implemented it in many churches. One of the more successful approaches was to host a pastors' breakfast. They would give out copies of the magazine and sign up as many of the pastors as they could to distribute them in their churches. Of course the church copies led to individual subscriptions as well. Within a year, the circulation had climbed rapidly from the plateau of twenty thousand to one hundred thousand copies each issue—the very number that Ken had prayed for on that cold Sunday afternoon.

Not all of Ken's projects were successful. While selling the books in the *Living* series, there was more money flowing in than they needed to pay salaries and bills. There was a healthy balance in the bank, and Ken felt that it should not stay there but rather be put to work. With some of the money, they launched a new periodical in 1967 called *Christian Times*, a weekly newspaper for adult Sunday school classes. It reported on Christian events and movements around the world. Ken thought it was one of the most terrific ideas he had ever had.

Christian Times seemed like a good way to make Christians more aware of God's work, which Ken hoped would make them more prayerful and increase their giving.

But he did no research. He did not analyze the costs of printing or promoting or maintaining circulation. They had enough money to support the newspaper until it got going, but unfortunately, budgets and cash flow projections were not done.

Ken's casual approach worked sometimes but not always. Two and a half years later, having lost $250,000 on *Christian Times*, Ken finally surrendered to reality, and the little newspaper was closed.

The story does not end there, however, because God did not let Ken's dream come to an end. A year later, while he was still nursing his personal pain and the financial disaster caused by the failure of *Christian Times*, God provided a new and practical way to achieve the original goal. Ken prepared a monthly news sheet called *The Church around the World*, designed to fit into church bulletins. He sent sample copies with order cards to thousands of pastors, who responded warmly. The monthly circulation grew, and by the end of 1976, they were mailing out more than a million copies of the little news sheet each month.

Out of disaster came great usefulness, but Ken often wondered why the disaster had to come first. He concluded that it was to destroy his pride and teach him valuable lessons in business. He had begun to think of himself as a successful businessman—something he wanted to be—but he needed to discover his shortcomings in that area. He had been impetuous about starting his pet project, assuming that anything he perceived as a need was obviously God's plan, as well. Nor had he counted the cost, as the New Testament counsels—and as a truly successful businessman would have remembered.

In 1968, while the *Christian Times* was still being published, another project began. It was a monthly tract called *Have a Good Day*. It is not an ordinary gospel tract, for the first three of its four pages are filled with items of human interest, heroism, inspiration, and trivia, plus some humorous cartoons. The back page carries an interesting, solid presentation of the good news of Christ. Ken called it the "non-tract" tract—a tract in purpose and result but not in format. Consequently, even timid Christians can give it away because no one is offended by being handed an attractive pamphlet called *Have a Good Day*. It is used by individuals and churches and by businesses owned by Christians who send it out with their monthly statements.

Another unique idea was also birthed in that era. One day, one of Tyndale's salesmen spoke with a manager of a J. C. Penney store in a small Midwestern city. This store was selling many *Living Bibles*, but the manager wanted to get a rackful of other Christian best-sellers, as well. The books he wanted came from a number of publishers, and he did not have time to contact all of them. And he knew that his small order would not generate any volume discount.

The Tyndale salesman solved the problem by buying books from the publishers, a few dozen copies at a time, and placing them on the rack in that one J. C. Penney store.

A few weeks later the results were in—that small

store was selling more than fifty Christian books a week. The salesman went on to call at J. C. Penney headquarters and got an order to supply dozens of their stores with the literature racks.

All the other publishers were eager to go along with the system and achieve a wider distribution of their books. Thus, Unirack was born—a name meaning one rack containing books from many publishers. Eventually the racks were in five hundred J. C. Penney stores, three hundred Kmart stores, many Montgomery Ward stores, and several other national chains.

In 1988 Tyndale's next periodical was launched, and it was a big one. Called *Dr. Dobson's Focus on the Family Bulletin*, it is a church bulletin insert drawn from materials published and produced by Dr. Dobson's Focus on the Family organization. At first Ken was not enthusiastic about the idea. He was afraid that it would cut into the circulation of *The Church around the World.* But his son Mark persisted with the idea of the new periodical, and after seeing a sample issue, Ken changed his mind. He was challenged by what he read and felt that many parents would be helped by it.

Demand for the bulletin quickly grew, and Tyndale House was soon sending out three million copies per month, without hurting the circulation of any other publication.

TWENTY-NINE

Financial Crisis

When *Living Letters* became popular all across America, Ken wondered if the people in England might have a similar interest in it. Ken made arrangements for *The Living New Testament* to be published by two major English publishers. After that, the entire *Living Bible* was readied for publication. The text was Anglicized for punctuation, colloquial words, and style. One major effort was to remove virtually all the exclamation points, which seemed inappropriate for the more reserved British reader. The British edition was released in 1974. An initial printing of two hundred thousand were all presold and immediately followed by reprints.

"Ken, what do you think about the bookstore business?" asked Bob Hawkins, the former bookstore owner who was now a member of the Tyndale sales team.

Ken thought for a while and replied, "Well, I'm all

for them. After all, how would we sell any of our books without them?"

"No," Bob said, "I mean how would you feel about Tyndale owning a bookstore or two?"

Ken thought it made sense, and Bob set about leasing retail space not far from the Tyndale offices. The store was an immediate success.

Buoyed by the success of the first store, Ken started planning a chain of Christian bookstores in the Chicago suburbs.

"We should go where the people are," he explained, "and set up stores in shopping malls."

He was soon faced with a stark reality. The high cost of setting up a store and paying incredibly high rent in malls put the concept at risk.

"It was beyond my expertise," Ken said.

But for some of these stores, it was too late. He had already signed leases in three other malls. Fortunately, by paying a stiff penalty, they were able to cancel two of the leases but went ahead with the third. The stores became a heavy financial drain on the company.

"But still," Ken countered, "thousands of lives are being helped by the Bibles and books we sold."

Another financial and almost fatal event occurred that same year when an opportunity to buy a Christian book distribution company came up. The company had been owned by the Multnomah School of the Bible in Portland. The business was of long standing and was quite successful.

Cash at Tyndale was readily available, since *The Living Bible* was selling at the rate of ten thousand copies per day.

And Ken felt good about purchasing the company, since it allowed the school to build a gymnasium.

They changed the name of the company to Unilit, short for "united literature," for their function was to buy books in cartons from a hundred or more publishers, store them in the Portland warehouse, and ship them to stores that ordered one or two or a dozen copies of any of the thousands of titles they carried. They shipped immediately, so that stores could have their orders within two or three days from one source. Up until then, the stores had to deal with hundreds of publishers, post hundreds of purchase orders, and have the books trickle in over weeks or months.

Unilit provided a wonderful service to stores, and Ken was the proud owner of the enterprise.

But Ken looked back and realized that while he prayed in all his activities and decisions, in the case of Unilit he asked the Lord to approve his decision rather than give him the proper direction. For some reason, this aspect of publishing was tantalizing to Ken, and he realized that his desire influenced his decisions.

"To use a football term," he explained, "flags were thrown down all over the field, but I kept running ahead."

Within a few months of buying the warehouse operation, Tyndale, under Ken's direction, opened another Unilit warehouse in southern California, then in Ohio, Georgia, and Texas, each with huge duplicate costs in inventory, warehouse space, and overhead. As a result, the profitable operation that he bought soon became a millstone around his neck and the neck of Tyndale House.

Ken's acquisitions didn't stop there. He had heard of an

opportunity in Sweden—a small Christian publishing firm needed fresh capital for growth. Sweden, like England, was a nation without much reliance on God; only about 4 percent of the population attended church. The small company in Sweden was profitable but always in need of money for expansion.

Meanwhile, back in America, Ken decided to discontinue the inexpensive, semiautomatic invoicing system at Tyndale. They transferred all their order processing and invoicing to the computer of a service bureau operated by a neighboring Christian organization. But their charges proved to be far more than Tyndale (or anyone else) could afford.

The financial clouds over Tyndale grew darker.

It was decided that Tyndale should bring all its computer work in-house, so the company purchased (on credit) a huge computer for five hundred thousand dollars—but had no software to run it. For additional hundreds of thousands of dollars, they developed the software they needed, but the programmers first needed to learn about publishing in order to program it correctly. They also bought a huge computer for Unilit and made the same mistake there.

Furthermore, when the computer finally was programmed, it was so slow that bookstores who wanted to order multiple items would sometimes be asked to wait a minute or more on the phone between items. Of course, they would not do that. The software vendor had guaranteed a two-second maximum wait, but there was no way to enforce the guarantee.

The consultant's face looked grim. Ken held his breath.

They had invited, and paid for, a consultant to come in and examine the operation.

"You have to send it back," he said seriously.

"Send what back?" Ken asked.

"The computer. The whole thing. You need to pay whatever penalty is involved."

"But what about the programming costs?"

"That's money down the drain," he concluded. "You need to bring in a microcomputer with software specifically designed for publishers."

It was a hard lesson to learn. The annual costs of computer expenses had dropped by hundreds of thousands of dollars—at least 80 percent. Yet Unilit was still saddled with the old computers.

A final blow to Unilit occurred when they extended unlimited credit to a friend who had developed a business of selling books in churches. The experiment, after months and months, did not work, and before anyone realized it, Tyndale was owed several hundred thousand dollars that would never be repaid.

Success of *The Living Bible* brought another sort of problem. Copies were selling at a fantastic rate, and Tyndale House was paying huge royalties into the Tyndale House Foundation. In Ken's zeal to get money into the foundation, he had written a royalty contract that was not economically feasible—and could not be changed for ten years.

Ken recalled sadly that other advisers had pleaded with him to reduce the royalty rate before he signed the agreement. But Ken did not listen to their advice. So Tyndale House could not keep up with its royalty obligations, and at one point it owed the foundation more than six million dollars in Bible royalties.

The bankers looked grim.

Ken and a few others had gathered in their office.

"We've reviewed your loan balances," the bankers said. "We don't like what we see. I'm afraid that our officers have demanded that you repay your loan of $2.8 million in thirty days."

Ken left in a state of shock. He had not realized how serious the financial condition of the company was. Now it was clear. Ken knew that they had to meet the demand. But if they did, they would be forced to declare bankruptcy. The bankers knew that, as well, but counseled that it was the safest course for all concerned.

Yet one banker believed in them. Jerry Bradshaw, from a local financial institution, convinced the other bankers that, given time, Tyndale would repay the loan. To monitor the company's progress, they set up an account that the bankers would control. All cash receipts would go into that account daily. They slowly began to pay back the loan. Part of that income was given back to Tyndale to pay salaries, printers, and all the other costs of doing business.

It took eighteen months to pay off the loan.

But by the time the bank claims had been met, Ken led the company into further entanglements. He had opened two more bookstores in expensive shopping malls, purchased the publishing house in Sweden, and opened a warehouse in Miami to export books to Latin America.

To complicate matters even further, Ken had been in Norway a few years earlier and had discovered a multivolume Christian encyclopedia that had captured his interest because of its strong sales in Norway and Sweden.

Ken recalled seeing dollar signs dancing in his head at the prospect of the encyclopedia. He admitted later that he greedily bought the U.S. publication rights. But upon closer scrutiny, Tyndale officials found the Norwegian material to be unsatisfactory, so they started over. They assembled a highly qualified group of scholars to contribute articles to an entirely new encyclopedia. The project was costing twenty thousand dollars per month—nearly a quarter of a million dollars per year.

Money flowed out into Ken's many projects, much of it never to return. At the end of 1977, he was hoping that Tyndale would show a small profit. But when employees counted the books in the warehouse and calculated their value, they were worth one million dollars less than they had earlier estimated. The manufacturing costs had not been entered correctly, and the financial reports and projections generated each month had all been wrong.

The company was in great trouble.

At the time, Ken realized that he needed advice, so he formed an outside board of directors to help oversee the workings of Tyndale. By paying close attention to overhead expenses and raising prices of Bibles and books, the company eked out a small profit in 1978. But Unilit and the encyclopedia were a continuing drain. Their financial problems were far from over. In fact, in 1979 they were getting worse.

"Ken, we need to talk," Margaret said. She was in charge of paying the bills at Tyndale House. "We're in trouble. . . . Tyndale is in trouble. I keep getting calls from all our vendors and suppliers. They demand getting paid. I can put them off for a while, but they're losing patience. And it isn't right for a Christian company to not pay its bills."

Ken was surprised. Margaret was usually the optimist.

But Margaret wasn't done. "It's clear to me that the company is on the verge of collapse," she said. "No one is facing the facts here. It seems like everyone is confused, helpless, or careless. This just can't go on."

That night, as the financial darkness deepened, Ken saw the bitter end in sight. He drove over to the Tyndale offices, alone, and poured out his heart to the living God. Ken tried his best to be open to the possibility that God had planned for Tyndale House to end in failure. But that idea was hard for Ken to accept.

Ken felt led by God that night. He stood in the middle of his office and prayed God's blessing on every part of it. Then he went through the building from office to office, praying specifically for God's blessing upon that particular work area. He walked around every one, claiming it as Joshua did as he went around the walls of Jericho. Ken claimed God's power against Satan, the destroyer, and asked God's blessings upon the inhabitants of Tyndale House. He spoke to the Lord about each person by name, and about his or her respective duties.

Slowly he made his way through the order entry department, the sales department, the credit department, the computer department, the production department, periodicals, editorial, customer service, and on and on. Then he went to the warehouse and put his head down on a carton of books and cried bitter tears.

Perhaps thirty minutes after he had completed his

tour, Ken was spiritually exhausted, hoping against hope, grasping for faith to move mountains, and feeling that there was nothing more that he could do.

Soon after, Margaret went to their son Mark's house and told him how serious she felt the situation had become. At the time, he was a vice president of the company. Margaret told Mark that some drastic steps had to be taken if the company was to be saved. Ken did not resent Margaret's move to get Mark involved.

A few days later, a trusted adviser called with the name of a bankruptcy attorney.

At this point, Mark, in effect, took charge. While Ken was traveling in Europe on business, Mark made the decision that Ken could not bring himself to make. He shut down the encyclopedia project with its quarter-of-a-million-dollar annual expense. He also sold a publishing company in England.

Mark continued by making some adjustments to the management team and squarely faced the management crisis in front of them. They spent time with bankers and set up rigid budgets. One department in the company had overspent its budget by two hundred thousand dollars the previous year. Ken had not complained, feeling the money had been well spent.

Mark's approach to the finances was simple: If the company did not have the money, then it would not spend it—no matter how worthwhile the purpose. Long discussions with their major bank brought about an extension of time and a payment schedule that the new austerity budget indicated they could meet.

Tyndale gave away its Swedish subsidiary. It had

been a financial drain, and they did not have the capital to keep it going. Tyndale also sold its company bookstores to Zondervan Corporation. In addition, they closed four of the five Unilit warehouses in 1975.

Within a few years, the growing cash-hungry and unprofitable divisions were gone from Tyndale and in stronger hands. A few years later, they sold the final Unilit warehouse and the Spanish language wholesaling division.

THIRTY

The Recent Past

Tyndale House Publishers made its way through the dark financial straits, and Ken assembled a team of skilled executives around him.

Over the next decade, distribution of Bibles, books, and magazines continued to increase, and more and more people were being reached for God by these materials. After Tyndale almost ceased to exist in the late 1970s, it has since operated profitably and has strengthened its financial base every year.

Mark Taylor, Ken's son, proved himself to be a skilled and capable executive during the difficult years. Ken began to think seriously of appointing him president of Tyndale.

One morning a Bible verse leapt out at Ken: "Now I will relieve your shoulder of its burden; I will free your hands from their heavy tasks" (Psalm 81:6 NLT). A few days later, in the spring of 1984, he asked Mark to become president and chief executive officer of Tyndale House Publishers, Inc.

At that time, Tyndale had around 190 employees—a long step up from the staff fitting around Ken's dining room table. Although the company had grown much, Ken always considered the staff family. Every year, he and Margaret graciously hosted a Christmas party for the entire Tyndale team and their guests. Since the gathering required a hotel or banquet facility, it couldn't be quite as homey as when Margaret could cook the entire Christmas meal. The Taylors also hosted a picnic for the Tyndale staff every summer.

Over the years, Tyndale has published many books for children, several of them written by Ken. To his great joy, the company formed a children's division that produced children's books by a variety of talented authors.

Of his writing of children's books, Ken said, "I hope the Lord will allow me to do this so my grandchildren will benefit from them. God has given me this particular gift, and I want to use it as long as possible. I believe that children read more than most adults and learn more from what they read. So I want Tyndale House to supply them with life-changing reading material."

In 1990 Tyndale moved south—one block south—to a new three-story, forty-thousand-square-foot building with a huge warehouse attached.

Ken attributed much of the increasing usefulness and financial progress of these more recent years to divine serendipities.

"A divine serendipity is an opportunity," he explained, "that came to Tyndale House unexpectedly and without our planning—even though they all required much hard work to bring them to final fruition."

One of these serendipities was a special edition of *The Living Bible* called *The Book*, used by Pat Robertson's Christian Broadcasting Network. Pat's purpose was to get people who had never read the Bible to become its readers. His plan was immensely successful, and several million copies of *The Book* went out across America in 1984 and 1985. It was advertised heavily on *The 700 Club* and on network television, reaching people who had never read the Bible before or who had tried to read older versions and had given up.

Another serendipity that seemed to come directly from God was the *One Year Bible*.

For several years, Ken had been asking God in prayer to tell him how to get more Christians to read His Word. He realized that many people had never read the Bible through even once. He knew from personal experience how easy it is to read through the books of Genesis and Exodus, then get bogged down and quit.

Ken mulled over the problem. Then he remembered that Billy Graham had once said that each day he tried to read some chapters from the Old Testament, some from the New Testament, a psalm or two, plus a few proverbs.

Ken recalled almost hearing God's voice say, "Why not publish a Bible with 365 daily sections—with each day's reading selected from those four parts of the Bible?"

Ken imagined that the opening page of this Bible would be headed January 1 and that day's reading would be the first chapter of Genesis, the first chapter of Matthew, the first Psalm, and the first few verses of

Proverbs. The reading for January 2 would include the next few chapters of those books, and so on, day by day, until December 31, when the entire Bible would have been read in the period of one year.

So Ken set to work. Cutting apart an old Bible, he pasted together a few sample pages in this dramatically different format. Ken convinced himself that the idea was practical and that it would take only fifteen minutes a day for the average reader to read through the entire Bible in one year.

"Surely anyone would be able to invest such a minimal amount of time to accomplish what they had always wanted to do—read the Bible through," said Ken.

The next week at a meeting with executives, he explained his idea: "Each day, the reader would get a little further in the Old Testament and the New Testament, plus Proverbs and Psalms."

There was silence around the table.

"But it's all jumbled up," one said.

"You mean that they don't just read from start to finish? What sort of logic is that?"

"I don't think anyone will buy it. It sounds too hard to explain."

Ken was dumbfounded. No one liked his idea. All of the team members were unanimous in their dissent. They felt that people simply would not use such an unusual organization of the Bible. The project was voted down, resoundingly.

But Ken was not deterred. He consulted a group of managers. His colleagues talked to Christian bookstores. They, too, were sure that it would never work.

People now remember with amusement the meeting

when the report from the bookstores was presented to Ken. The publication committee was relieved that the matter was settled and that Tyndale would not proceed.

Mark, then the president of the company, explained the many reasons why Ken should forget it and asked for his father's agreement to drop the matter.

Ken looked stern. "No. Let's go ahead with it."

They decided on the title *The One Year Bible*.

Since that time, several million copies have been distributed, in many different Bible translations. Hundred and thousands of people have written saying that they have read through the Bible for the first time in their lives and how grateful they are to Tyndale House Publishers for helping them in this task.

Yet another divinely planned but hard-earned serendipity came a few years later, before anyone at Tyndale House knew about it.

The director of publishing at Youth for Christ U.S.A. saw the need for an entirely new kind of study Bible—not one with notes that explain the meaning of a verse, but one with notes that apply a verse to everyday Christian living. These notes would answer the question, "What does this verse teach us about how we should live our lives?"

No such study Bible was available, so the director set out to create one. He called upon scores of Youth for Christ leaders to find "life applications" from verses in each chapter throughout the entire Bible. Writing the notes required thousands of hours of research and hard work.

When the project was complete, the director said that no text other than *The Living Bible* was suitable for the project. Tyndale House enthusiastically agreed to publish this new study Bible and called it the Life Application Bible.

This Bible has been enormously helpful to its readers and is now available in many different translations. Millions of copies are in print, and the notes are being translated into other languages for worldwide use.

One more delightful serendipity was the children's video series *McGee and Me!* that is now in millions of homes. The project started when a large foundation was asked to help fund a Bible translation project for Living Bibles International. It soon became evident that the foundation's greater interest was to provide outstanding Christian video material for children in America.

"Why are Christians unable to produce children's videos of top professional quality?" they asked.

Tyndale executives knew that they could be produced, but the costs were prohibitive—then in the neighborhood of four hundred thousand dollars for a half-hour video.

The foundation said, "If you can find top-quality people to produce truly top-quality videos that communicate biblical values, we will pay for it."

So Living Bibles International, Focus on the Family, and Tyndale House Publishers teamed up to produce these programs.

Within two years, a million copies of the *McGee and Me!* videos had been distributed.

It was a wonderful idea—and once again Tyndale was God's chosen instrument to make it all come true.

A revision of *The Living Bible* became a major project at

Tyndale. Decades before, when *The Living Bible* was first published in one volume, Ken knew that it would need to be updated every few years to reflect changes in language usage and to correct any verses that did not adequately express the original Greek and Hebrew texts.

For several years, with all the rush and excitement of the immense popularity and distribution of *The Living Bible*, this revision did not happen. Then Ken spent years on a revision, only to recognize that it did not improve the original *Living Bible* text.

In 1986 staff proposed a different way of accomplishing Ken's goal of complete accuracy. They suggested that Tyndale find a group of top Christian scholars to identify the verses that needed improvement, and then Ken, along with other stylists, could work with the scholars to retranslate those verses.

It was a wonderful idea, far better than Ken's trying to identify the inadequate verses by himself. So he tossed aside his many years of solo work and began working with a team of the best evangelical scholars in the English-speaking world.

In 1996, exactly twenty-five years after the release of *The Living Bible*, Tyndale House Publishers released the *Holy Bible*, New Living Translation.

Accolades and strong appreciation for this new translation have come from all corners of the religious world. And it appears that it has accomplished what Ken had always hoped to achieve in terms of accuracy and readability.

EPILOGUE

This manuscript was drawn largely from Ken Taylor's autobiography *My Life: A Guided Tour,* which he finished in 1991. Mark Taylor, Ken's son and current president at Tyndale House, wrote the following thoughts eleven years later:

> As I write in the fall of 2002, my parents continue to be very active at the age of eighty-five. My father still puts in full days at Tyndale House. My mother maintains an active lifestyle as homemaker and hostess to friends and family. They still live in the "new house" they built in 1966 at the site of the old farmhouse in Wheaton.
>
> Their twenty-eighth grandchild was born in 1992. As of this writing, eight of the grandchildren are married, and there are now fifteen great-grandchildren. The immediate family numbers seventy, with two more on the way.

*Tyndale House is celebrating its fortieth anniversary this year. We've come a long way from the dining room and the garage. In 2001, for instance, the best-selling novel in America was a Tyndale title (*Desecration*—the ninth book in the Left Behind series). In 2002, two different Tyndale titles hit #1 on the* New York Times *best-seller list, one in fiction (*The Remnant*) and one in nonfiction (*Let's Roll*). And we believe that the numerical success points to success in fulfilling our corporate purpose: "To minister to the spiritual needs of people, primarily through literature consistent with biblical principles."*

On June 10, 2005, after eighty-eight years on this earth, Ken Taylor died at his Wheaton, Illinois, home. The husband, father, businessman, author, and Bible translator moved on to his heavenly home and eternal reward.

Just a few months earlier, Ken had anticipated his own death in an article he wrote for *Wheaton*, the alumni magazine of Wheaton College. Figuring that he had no more than two or three more years to live, Ken predicted that few people would dwell on his passing, other than to say, "Sorry to hear it." That thought was, in Ken's words, "a reminder to me that we do not live for praise but to help others, so whatever needs doing must be done now."

Ken Taylor may have underestimated the response to his own death, but his assessment of spiritual service was right on target. Ken's lifetime of faithfulness to God—fully supported by his wife, Margaret—was summed up by his son Mark in comments that should challenge each one of us to similar obedience:

As I look back over my parents' lives, I am impressed by all that they have done. But even more impressive is the attitude with which they have done it. God gave them a task to do, and they did it willingly. He gave them small resources, and they used them wisely. At various points along the way he said, "Well done, My good and faithful servants. You have been faithful in handling this small amount, so now I will give you many more responsibilities." And someday, when they stand before the Lord, they will hear him say, "Well done, my good and faithful servant[s]. . . . Let's celebrate together!" (Matthew 25:21 NLT).

The challenge continues, and each generation is given new opportunities for service, more opportunities to be salt and light in a world in need. I trust that my generation will be as faithful as my parents in carrying out the work God has given us.

FOR FURTHER READING

Taylor, Kenneth N., and Virginia Muir. *My Life: A Guided Tour—The Autobiography of Kenneth N. Taylor.* Wheaton, IL: Tyndale House Publishers, 1991.

Taylor, Kenneth N. "On Aging." *Wheaton,* Autumn 2004, 14.